"We feel that for too long our leaders have used politics as the art of the possible.
The challenge now is to practice politics as the art of making what appears to be impossible, possible..."
Hillary Rodham (later Clinton)
Wellesley College student body president delivering a graduation address, May 1969.

REMEMBERING THE LADIES:
FROM PATRIOTS IN PETTICOATS
TO PRESIDENTIAL CANDIDATES

Courageous and Tenacious American Women
Not JUST a Coloring Book
by Carol Simon Levin

Illustrated by
Aarti Arora, Aditi Tandon, Aileen Wu, Amber McGonegal, Arlene Holmes, Barbara Schneider, Caroline Mack, Caroline Yorke, Crina Magalio, Diana Patton, Holly Bess Kincaid, Jasmine Florentine, Jen Wistuba, Jill Obrig, Jill Schmidt, Jody Flegal, Judy Hnat, Julie Goetz, Justine Turnbull, Kat Schroeder, Kim Defibaugh, Kim Wood, Laura Leigh Myers, Laura Davidson, Lena Shiffman, Leslie Simon, Lynnor Bontigao, Mariya Kovalyov, Mary Delaney Connelly, Monisha Kulkarni, Natalie Obedos, Rachel Wintemberg, Sheryl Depp, Tiffany Castle, Tish Wells, and Victoria Ford.

A Telling Her Stories Production Tellingherstories.com

2nd Edition

D1404280

Dedication:

It has been my privilege to work with this dedicated team of talented illustrators
who helped bring to life the many women who toiled tirelessly to achieve equal rights
and better conditions for women and children, people of color, immigrants and the poor.

Thank you to all who pledged to the Kickstarter and provided the initial funding to make this book a reality.

This book is also dedicated to the dream of a
National Women's History Museum
(currently only an online museum nwhm.org)
in the hope that someday it will join
The National Museum of American History
The National Museum of the American Indian
and the newly-opened
National Museum of African American History and Culture
as a Smithsonian Museum on the National Mall.

More thanks than I can possibly express to **Laura Davidson for designing the lovely logo** for the project and
Mariya Kovalyov for her beautiful cover, to Lori Rosolowsky and Eve Simon for their extensive editing assistance,
and most of all to my husband, Gary, who provided invaluable technical support and patience!
–Carol Simon Levin

Fair Use: You are welcome to make photocopies of individual pages to try different coloring schemes or share
with friends and to post your finished images to social media – a link to the coloring book is always appreciated!
Teachers, youth leaders, librarians, coloring group coordinators and others may make multiple copies of a limited
number of pages to share with their group – again please share the source of the pages. If you plan to use a
substantial number of pages, please purchase a copy for each participant. Discount bulk rates are available.
Contact me at rememberingtheladies.book@gmail.com for details.

Accuracy: In a work of this scope, despite my best efforts, I am bound to have made errors – if you spot any,
please email me at rememberingtheladies.book@gmail.com so I can correct them in future printings.

They called it "Freedom" by Zack Applewhite

Free to speak ~~our minds~~
Of children
And what's for dinner

Free to work ~~for ourselves~~
Around the house
And on the garden

Free to learn ~~real knowledge~~
French
And how to sew

Free to know ~~our rights~~
What soap to buy
And what's on sale

Free to vote ~~our interests~~
At PTA meetings
And church functions

...

Free to earn ~~equal wages~~
"Enough" money
And the "respect" of others

Free to feel ~~safe at work~~
Staring eyes
And grazing hands

Free to wear ~~empowering clothes~~
Long skirts
And high necklines

...

Free to Fight **_For Our Freedom_**
With husbands
And friends

Poem from:
kickstarter.com/projects/bettagam
es/the-1-poem-project

Cartoon by Lou Rogers
from **Judge** magazine 1912
(Creative Commons Public Domain)

TEARING OFF THE BONDS.

Welcome!

Whether you are 8 or 108, I hope you will enjoy this unusual coloring book which not only gives you images to color but also an introduction to many courageous and tenacious American women who have promoted the rights and improved the lives of women and those in need.

In this coloring book, I have endeavored to share some of them, but space and time precluded me from covering everyone I would have liked, thoroughly telling their stories, or telling them in a way that is most accessible to young people.

I hope, however, that this book encourages you to follow the "read more" and "visit" links to seek out more information on these fascinating and sometimes forgotten women.

Please visit **tellingherstories.com** for Information about performances of "Remembering the Ladies" and my other historical impersonation programs and to find out about other upcoming books in this series.

A note about names:

It is customary in conventional journalism to refer to people by their last names. But for most women, those last names changed after their marriages and belonged to their fathers and husbands. So instead I have chosen to use their first names – names most retained throughout their lives.

Table of Contents:

Founding Mothers:

Abolitionists and Suffragists:

- Carrie Chapman Catt (1859-1947) – Leader of the National Woman Suffrage Association and Founder of the League of Women Voters

- Anna Howard Shaw (1847-1919) – Powerful Speaker for the Women's Suffrage Movement

- Harriot Stanton Blatch (1856-1940) – Working Class Suffrage Organizer

- Inez Milholland (1886 –1916) – "White Knight" and Martyr for the Women's Suffrage Movement

- Alice Paul (1885-1977) – Feminist, Suffragist, and Political Strategist

Advocates for Worker, Immigrant, Women's and Civil rights:

- Emma Lazarus (1849-1887) – Poet and Activist for Immigrant Rights

- Ida Bell Wells-Barnett (1862-1931) – African-American Journalist and Anti-Lynching Activist

- Mary Church Terrell (1863-1954) – Suffrage Activist and First President of the National Association of Colored Women

- Nellie Bly (1864-1922) – Investigative Journalist who Wrote Exposé on Women Falsely Institutionalized for Madness

- Juliette Gordon Low (1860-1927) – Founded the Girl Scouts of America with the Goal of Helping Girls Become Independent and Self-Reliant

- Margaret Sanger (1883-1966) – Thrown in Jail in 1916 after Opening the First U.S. Birth-Control Clinic

- Rose Schneiderman (1884-1972) – Labor Organizer and Founder of the Ladies Garment Workers Association.

- Elizabeth Gurley Flynn (1890-1964) – "Rebel Girl" and "East Side Joan of Arc"

- Francis Perkins (1880-1965) – Secretary of Labor and First Woman Cabinet Minister in the U.S. Government

- Zitkala-Ša (1876–1938) – Native American and Women's Rights Activist

- Elouise Pepion Cobell (1945-2011) – Tribal Activist who Worked to Restore Funds Owed to Native Americans

- Rosa Parks (1913-2005) – "The First Lady of Civil Rights"

- Septima Poinsette Clark (1898-1987) – "Freedom's Teacher"

- Ella Baker (1903-1986) – "Unsung Heroine of the Civil Rights Movement"

- Fannie Lou Hamer (1917-1977) – African American Voting and Civil Rights Activist

- Dolores Huerta (1930-) – Labor Leader, Women's and Migrant Rights Advocate

- Betty Friedan (1921-2006) – Groundbreaking Author of the 1963 Book *The Feminine Mystique* Which Kicked off a New Wave of Feminism

- Gloria Steinem (1934-) – Founder of Ms. Magazine and Outspoken Champion for Women's Rights

- Marian Wright Edelman (1939-) – Founder of the Children's Defense Fund

A Woman's Place is in the House...and the Senate! The Supreme Court, The State Department and Tribal Government

- Jeannette Rankin (1880-1973) –"I may be the first woman member of Congress but I won't be the last"

- Patsy Mink (1927-2002) – The First Asian American Woman Elected to Congress

- Bella Abzug (1920-1998) – "Battling Bella" Outspoken Liberal Activist and Politician Who Introduced the First Gay Rights Bill in Congress

- Patricia Schroeder (1940-) – Congresswoman Known for Her Witty and Biting One-Liners

- Barbara Jordan (1936-1996) – Black Congresswoman Who was Called "The Conscience of the Nation"

- Sandra Day O'Connor (1930-) – First Woman Supreme Court Justice

- Ruth Bader Ginsberg (1933-) – "Sister in Law"

- Sonia Sotomayor (1954-) – First Latina Supreme Court Justice

- Madeleine Albright (1937-) – First Woman to Become U.S. Secretary of State "The Most Powerful Woman in the World"

- Wilma Mankiller (1945-2010) – First Woman Chief of the Cherokee Nation

- Nancy Pelosi (1940-) – First Woman to Become Speaker of the House

- Elizabeth Warren (1949-) – Feisty Democratic Senator and Consumer Advocate

The Road to the White House:

- Victoria Woodhull (1838-1937) – First Woman to Run for President of the United States

- Belva Lockwood (1830-1917) – First Woman Lawyer to Argue before the Supreme Court, Second Woman to Run for President

- Edith Bolling Wilson (1872-1961) – Rumored to be Acting President of the United States

- Eleanor Roosevelt (1884-1962) – First Lady to the World and Champion of Human Rights

- Margaret Chase Smith (1897-1995) – First Female Senator Elected in Her Own Right and the First Woman to Seek the Nomination of a Major Political Party (Republican)

- Lady Bird Johnson (1912-2007) – Environmentalist and Activist First Lady

- Shirley Chisholm (1924-2005) – First Black Congresswoman and First African American Woman to Run for President

- Rosalynn Carter (1927-) – "More a Political Partner than a Political Wife"

- Geraldine Ferraro (1935-2011) – First Female Vice Presidential Candidate from a Major American Political Party

- Hillary Rodham Clinton (1947-) – First Woman Nominee for President from a Major Political Party

Founding Mothers – Patriots in Petticoats:

- Abigail Adams (1744-1818) – "Remember the Ladies"

- Eliza Lucas Pinckney (1722-1793) – "Indigo Girl" Teenage Entrepreneur and Revolutionary Financier

- Mercy Otis Warren (1728-1814) –   Female Historian and Propagandist of the American Revolution Who Helped Spur Passage of the Bill of Rights

- Mary Katherine Goddard (1738-1816) – Postmistress and Publisher of the Declaration of Independence

- Martha Washington (1731-1802) – Partner in the Revolution

- Dolley Madison (1768-1849) – "Queen Dolley"   Masterful Behind-the-Scenes Politician

- Sacagawea (c 1790-?) – First Native American Woman Accorded the Right to Vote in an Official U.S. Government Venture

Abigail Adams (1744-1818)   "Remember the Ladies"

Like most other girls of her time, Abigail had little formal education – something she minded a great deal – yet Abigail's letters show that she was widely-read and had a great deal of common sense and courage. Her knowledge of classical literature, history, and French was evident in the more than 1100 letters she would send her husband, John, during their 54-year-long marriage – many of those years spent apart while he served the new country, first in the Continental Congress and then as the new country's representative in Paris. Her letters included family stories, but also financial reports of the farm she was managing in his absence, news of the war around their home in Massachusetts and political suggestions. However, her famous plea asking that the Continental Congress "remember the ladies" as they drafted the new laws was completely ignored – John wrote back amused that she was "so saucy."

John Adams was a 23-year-old country lawyer when 14-year-old Abigail first got to know him. He was impressed by her knowledge of poetry, philosophy and politics. She, by his energy, intelligence, and enthusiasm. As he became active in revolutionary politics, she eagerly encouraged him – even though it meant he was absent from home for long periods and she was left alone to tend their farm and children. In 1778, the Continental Congress sent John Adams to Paris to arrange French assistance for the struggling new country. The country was at war and Great Britain controlled the seas, capturing ships and dumping correspondence. Abigail went for months not knowing if her husband was even alive. Finally in 1784, he sent for her and she and her oldest daughter sailed for France. The ship provided passage but little else. She had to provide all their food for the month-long journey – including chickens for eggs and a cow for milk! She also brought bedding and linens – a sheet was hung from a clothesline to separate their cabin area from that of the crew – as well as gallons of vinegar and a box of medicines to try to clean the ship and stave off illness.

In 1789, John Adams became the new nation's first Vice President and then President in 1797 after George Washington refused to run for a third term. Abigail continued to discuss political issues with her husband and often gave him candid advice. Critics accused her of "meddling" and many of John's political opponents ridiculed him for being under the thumb of a "Mrs. President."

They spent most of his term in the temporary capital in Philadelphia, then moved into the new presidential mansion in Washington, DC for the last three months of his presidency. Conditions were difficult – Abigail wrote that *"not one room or chamber is finished...It is habitable by fires in every part, thirteen of which we are obliged to keep daily, or sleep in wet and damp places."* She hung laundry in what is now the East Room. After Thomas Jefferson defeated John Adams in his bid for re-election, Abigail and John happily returned to their home in Quincy. Abigail died in 1818, seven years before her eldest son, John Quincy Adams, became the nation's sixth president.

Fascinating Factoid: The U.S. Constitutional Convention gave states the right to decide on voting qualifications and at the time one state – New Jersey – allowed women to vote. A 1776 New Jersey law had given the vote to all adults with property over a certain value. Married women couldn't vote because the husband technically owned the property, but single women and widows could and did – a 1790 New Jersey law even referred to voters as "he or she." But when a large number of women voted in the 1800 presidential election (in which Jefferson defeated John Adams), the legislature decided to change the law and in 1807, voting was confined to white men.

Read More – *for Kids:* **Who Was Abigail Adams?** by True Kelley, 2014. *for Teens and Adults:* **My Dearest Friend: Letters of Abigail and John Adams** by Abigail Adams and John Adams (or other editions of her letters). **Abigail Adams** by Woody Holton, 2009. **John Adams** by David McCullough, 2001. (Feather Foster writes of Abigail's journey to Paris here: featherfoster.wordpress.com/2013/08/05/mrs-adams-goes-to-paris)

Visit: Adams National Historical Park, Quincy, MA. www.nps.gov/adam/index.htm

Abigail Adams (1744-1818) by Crina Magalio © 2016 crinamagalioillustration.blogspot.com

"And by the way in the new Code of Laws...I desire you would remember the ladies, and be more generous...to them than your ancestors... If particular care and attention is not paid to the ladies, we are determined to foment a rebellion and will not hold ourselves bound by any Laws in which we have no voice or Representation." – Abigail Adams, writing to her husband John at the Continental Congress on March 31, 1776

Eliza Lucas Pinckney (1722-1793)   "Indigo Girl"
Teenage Entrepreneur and Revolutionary Financier

Imagine being a sixteen-year-old girl in 1738 and being put in charge of three enormous rice plantations because your father has left the country and your mother is ill…

Imagine experimenting with the indigo plant, patiently growing and processing the blue dye through frost and failure and then seeing it, just a few years later, become your colony's biggest money maker…

Imagine importing cocoons from China, growing silkworms, harvesting the silk, and giving one of the dresses made from that fabric to the King of England's mother…

Imagine becoming a mother to two American patriots who fought in the Revolutionary War – one who helped write the Constitution; the other who became Governor of South Carolina and, when you died, having your coffin carried to your grave by President George Washington.

Born in the colonial West Indies and educated in England, Eliza Lucas Pinckney was the daughter of George Lucas, a lieutenant-colonel in the British army. In 1738, he moved the family from Antigua to South Carolina when he inherited three plantations near Charleston. When her father was recalled to Antigua to fight in the strangely-named "War of Jenkins Ear" a month before her seventeenth birthday, Eliza Lucas found herself in charge of three failing rice plantations covering an area of more than 5,000 acres – seven square miles – nearly 4,000 football fields! Eliza was now both plantation master & mistress – overseeing the crops and the business of the plantations but also overseeing everything done in the house and gardens. She wrote to her father about local political and military news, business transactions of money and crops on the three plantations, and discussed the efficient use of their eighty-six Carolina "servants" (she didn't use the term "slaves.") Eliza set up a schoolroom to give her little sister Polly daily lessons. Despite a 1740 South Carolina law prohibiting teaching slaves to read, Eliza decided to include two black girls in her schoolroom so that they might teach the rest of the "Negroe children" on her plantation. By the age of 22, through extensive experimentation, despite crop failures and deliberate sabotage, she had figured out how to grow, harvest and produce dye from the indigo plant – even though nearly every other colonial farmer had thought it was impossible. That crop soon became colonial South Carolina's biggest moneymaker – by 1754, South Carolina was exporting more than a million pounds a year to England!

Eliza was always thinking up "little schemes" (as she called them) for making money. As a teenager, she planted oak trees certain that someday the colonies would want the wood for ships. They did! In 1744, after she married the lawyer Charles Pinckney, she imported silkworm cocoons from China, grew the worms, unwound the silk and, when she went to England, presented a gown made from that fabric to the King's Mother. And during the Revolutionary War, she loaned her fortune –£4000 pounds (the equivalent of at least a half a million dollars in today's money) to the South Carolina army. When she died, George Washington insisted on carrying her coffin.

Fascinating Factoid: In addition to her other accomplishments, Eliza dabbled in law: *"We have some in this Neighborhood who have a little Land and a few slaves and Cattle to give their children that never think of making a will till they come upon a sick bed and find it too expensive to send to town for a Lawyer. If You will not laugh too immoderately at me I'll Trust you with a secret. I have made two wills already. I know I have done no harm for I coned [learned] my lesson very perfect and know how to convey by will Estates real and personal and never forget in its proper place, him and his heirs for Ever, nor that 'tis to be signed by 3 Witnesses …."*

Read More – *for Kids:* **Founding Mothers: Remembering the Ladies** by Cokie Roberts, 2014. *for Teens and Adults:* **Founding Mothers: The Women Who Raised Our Nation** by Cokie Roberts, 2004. **Letterbook of Eliza Lucas Pinckney, 1739-1762: Intriguing Letters by One of Colonial America's Most Accomplished Women** by Eliza Lucas Pinckney and Marvin R. Zahnise, 1997. **Eliza Pinckney** by H. H. Ravenel, 1896. **Eliza Lucas Pinckney: Colonial Plantation Manager and Mother of American Patriots 1722-1793** by Margaret F. Pickett, 2016.

Visit: Eliza's silk dress is on view at the **Smithsonian National Museum of American History** in Washington, DC
americanhistory.si.edu/american-stories/1776-1801-forming-new-nation

Eliza Lucas Pinckney (1722-1793) "Indigo Girl" by Tiffany Castle © 2016
Teenage Entrepreneur and Revolutionary Financier

"Wont you laugh at me if I tell you I am so busy in providing for Posterity
I hardly allow myself time to Eat or sleep...
I am making a large plantation of Oaks which I look upon as my own property,
whether my father gives me the land or not; and therefore I design many years hence when oaks are more
valuable than they are now —which you know they will be when we come to build fleets." --1741

Mercy Otis Warren (1728-1814)
Female Historian and Propagandist of the American Revolution Who Helped Spur Passage of the Bill of Rights

On November 15, 1775, seven months after Lexington and Concord and three months after King George III declared the colonies in a state of rebellion, Mercy Warren was impatient with the slow and cautious deliberations of the Continental Congress. As her husband James reported in a letter to their friend the delegate John Adams: *"She [Mrs. Warren] sits at the table with me, will have a paragraph of her own; says you [Congress] "should no longer piddle at the threshold. It is time to leap into the theatre, to unlock the bars, and open every gate that impedes the rise and growth of the American republic, and then let the giddy potentate send forth his puerile proclamations to France, to Spain and all the commercial world who may be united in building up an Empire which he can't prevent."*

Mercy got her first taste of politics from the stories she heard from her father, a traveling lawyer and member of the Massachusetts House of Representatives. She convinced him to allow her to study languages, history, philosophy, and literature alongside her two older brothers as they prepared to enter Harvard. Mercy couldn't follow them to Harvard – colleges wouldn't admit girls – but devoured the books her brothers brought home and ended up marrying one of their friends, a farmer and politician named James Warren. Mercy read the political thoughts of John Locke regarding freedom and "natural rights" and became convinced of the injustice of British rule. She and her husband became good friends of John and Abigail Adams, Sam Adams, and John Hancock – and their parlor became a meeting point of ideas regarding American resistance. Noting her classical education and talent with words, John Adams encouraged Mercy to write patriotic poems and plays ridiculing British policies and Loyalist supporters. These were published anonymously in the papers throughout the colonies and she became one of the most influential propagandists of her time. After war broke out in Massachusetts, Mercy sent letters to the Continental Congress and General George Washington describing British warships and enemy atrocities in Boston and urged them to send soldiers.

Mercy corresponded with Abigail and John Adams, Martha Washington, Thomas Jefferson, Patrick Henry, Alexander Hamilton and other early leaders. In early 1775, with encouragement from John Adams, she decided to write a history of the American Revolution and she actively began to coerce her correspondents to send her accounts of debates in Congress, copies of correspondence and any other information they could supply. When her three volume **History of the Rise, Progress, and Termination of the American Revolution** was finally published thirty years later, President Thomas Jefferson ordered copies for himself and for every member of his cabinet. Mercy wrote an essay in 1788 opposing the proposed Constitution because she felt it should guarantee more individual liberties, including freedom of the press. Her arguments helped spur passage of the first ten amendments to the Constitution in 1791, which came to be known as the "Bill of Rights." Though Mercy didn't advocate formal political rights for women, her writings argued that women could inspire their countrymen to action and she is considered America's first female historian.

Fascinating Factoid: The famous phrase *"Taxation without representation is tyranny"* was written by James Otis, one of Mercy's brothers. Another famous phrase *"Give Me Liberty!"* inspired the slave Elizabeth Freeman (or Mum Bet) to sue for her own freedom. In 1781, Mum Bet found a lawyer who would argue her case under the new Massachusetts Constitution which stated that "all men are born free and equal." She won her own freedom plus monetary compensation for beatings she had received and her case helped lead to Massachusetts outlawing slavery in 1783.

Read More – *for Kids:* **Write on Mercy! The Secret Life of Mercy Otis Warren** by Gretchen Woelfle, 2012. *for adults:* **The Muse of the Revolution: The Secret Pen of Mercy Otis Warren and the Founding of a Nation** by Nancy Rubin Stuart, 2009.

Visit: Mercy Warren Otis Statue outside the Barnstable County Courthouse, Barnstable MA

MRS. MERCY WARREN

Mercy Otis Warren (1728-1814)   Abner D. Jones, ed., *The Illustrated American Biography*, vol. 3 (1855), p. 107.
Articulate Advocate for Individual Rights and Historian of the American Revolution.

"The rights of the individual should be the primary object of all governments."

Mary Katherine Goddard (1738-1816)
First Female Postmistress and Publisher of the Declaration of Independence

Mary was introduced to the printing business and postal system through her family. Her father was a physician and postmaster of New London, Connecticut. After he died, Mary's mother Sarah moved the family to Providence, Rhode Island and loaned her son William the money to begin a printing business publishing the **Providence Gazette**. Since William traveled a great deal, Sarah ended up being the acting publisher and Mary worked as typesetter, printer, and journalist. The mother/daughter team made their print shop a great success and they added a bookbindery as well. They repeated this arrangement after William moved to Philadelphia in 1765. After Sarah died in 1770, Mary kept the business running when her brother was jailed for writing inflammatory articles in the paper and for public outbursts. The shop became one of the most successful in the colonies. In 1773, William moved again – this time to start a paper in Baltimore. Mary then managed the Baltimore paper while William set up an inter-colonial postal system separate from the official British one. On May 10, 1775, Mary officially adopted the title of publisher of the **Maryland Journal and the Baltimore Advertiser**. She put "Published by M.K. Goddard" on the masthead. That year Mary also became the first female postmaster in colonial America –initially serving under the official leadership of Postmaster General Benjamin Franklin – which also gave her paper access to the news ahead of its competitors.

After the Declaration of Independence was signed in Philadelphia on July 4, 1776, a few printed copies were circulated throughout the new nation without the signers' names. On January 18, 1777, the Second Continental Congress moved that the Declaration of Independence be widely distributed, and Mary offered the use of her press in spite of the risks – it was considered a treasonable document by the British. Sadly in 1784, Mary Katherine's name disappeared from the **Journal**. It is believed that William, unsuccessful at his own businesses, forced his sister to quit. She remained a successful postmaster for 14 years but, in 1789, she was forced out by Postmaster General Samuel Osgood who claimed a woman could not handle the traveling the job would soon demand. Mary appealed to George Washington and the Congress about the injustice and over 200 Baltimore businessmen presented a petition demanding her reinstatement, but her petition failed. She spent the rest of her life running a bookstore in Baltimore.

Fascinating Factoid: During the American Revolution, newspapers became essential forms of communication. Even though money was tight, Mary never missed publishing an edition of the paper from 1775 to 1784. She accepted food as payment for the paper and she kept the mail going – sometimes using her own money to pay post riders.

Deborah Read Franklin "Ben's Right-Hand (Wo) Man" (c1708 -1774) was also a female printer and postmistress. Deborah met Ben Franklin when they were both in their teens and Ben was an apprentice printer, then again when Ben returned from England and opened a printing shop at the back of her mother's store. Ben was often busy with his newspaper and inventions, so Deborah ran both shops. When the stamp act passed, Philadelphia colonists were angry that Ben hadn't stopped it and showed up to attack their house. Deborah and her relatives held off the mob with guns. Ben praised her *"spirit and courage"* but didn't come back home despite her pleas.

Read More – *for Kids:* **Founding Mothers: Remembering the Ladies** by Cokie Roberts, 2014. *for Adults:* **Founding Mothers: The Women Who Raised Our Nation** by Cokie Roberts, 2004. **Enterprising Women 250 Years of American Business** by Virginia G. Drachman , 2002 (this book also features a profile of Eliza Pinckney and another great female newspaper publisher, Katharine Graham, owner of the Washington Post Company.)

Visit: National Postal Museum Washington, DC www. postalmuseum.si.edu
Independence Park and **Ben Franklin Museum** Philadelphia, PA www.nps.gov/inde

Mary Katherine Goddard (1738-1816) by Caroline Mack © 2016 www.carolinemackdesign.com
Postmistress and Publisher of the Declaration of Independence

"She, therefore, most humbly hopes from your Excellency's Philanthropy and wonted Humanity,
You will take her Situation into Consideration; and as the Grievance complained of,
has happened whilst the Post Office Department was put under your auspicious Protection,
by a Resolve of Congress, that Your Excellency will be graciously pleased to order, that She may be restored to her
former Office, and as in duty bound, She will ever pray..." – Petition t**o George Washington from Mary Katherine**
Goddard, 23 December 1789

Martha Washington (1731-1802)   Partner in the Revolution

The United States was a new country, but its laws were no friendlier to women than those in the European countries. Women were considered property, first belonging to their fathers, then their husbands. Educational opportunities were limited, they couldn't vote or have any official role in government – indeed America's founding fathers believed that women in politics would be completely unnatural *"a world turned upside down."*

Martha Washington was a wealthy widow in charge of a large plantation when she married George Washington in 1759. After their marriage, she and her two children moved into Mount Vernon, Washington's plantation. When Washington left to become General of the Revolutionary Army, Martha divided her time between managing the plantation and traveling to the army's winter encampments, supporting her husband and the soldiers emotionally and with clothing and other physical comforts.

"I never in my life knew a woman so busy from early morning until late at night as was Lady Washington," remarked a visitor to Valley Forge. In that terrible winter when troops were freezing, starving and sick, Martha Washington was invaluable in preventing desertion. She and other officers' wives sewed, cooked, nursed, entertained, and were loved by the troops. In total, she spent eight long winters during the war at military camps. In addition, Martha Washington volunteered to get the smallpox vaccine even though it was a live vaccine and potentially deadly so that the soldiers would be willing to get inoculated (without which the Americans might have lost the war).

After the war was over, Martha was eager to return to a private life in Mount Vernon, but the country had other ideas. When her husband was elected President in 1789, she said she felt like a state prisoner because he considered it inappropriate for her to go out to public places and private residences in New York City (the nation's first capital). So she and Abigail Adams (the wife of the Vice President) held Friday night gatherings each week open to any and all "respectable" persons. After her husband's presidency ended, Martha and George returned to Mount Vernon, where Martha hosted literally hundreds of visitors every year. She was known to have an amazing memory for faces and people's stories and some historians credit her social skills as greatly contributing to the popularity of her husband's presidency.

Catharine Littlefield Greene (Caty/Kitty) (1754-1814) was another impressive "Patriot in Petticoats." Like Martha, Caty traveled to her husband's military camp nearly every year (often with a new baby in tow). General Nathanael Green died soon after the war was over, and Catharine fought for Congress to pay back money her husband had spent on clothing for his soldiers. When she finally won, her friend President George Washington signed the bill into law. Incidentally, Eli Whitney was a toolmaker on her plantation and invented the cotton gin in a laboratory at her house, most likely at her suggestion. Catherine financed the patent and fabrication of the cotton gin ("gin" being short for "engine") and there is also some evidence that she solved some of the gin's initial design flaws. However women at the time were not allowed to hold patents and, though Eli Whitney paid her royalties on the patent, Catherine was given no public credit.

Fascinating Factoid: Martha Washington was the first American woman to have her portrait on paper money (1886) and on a stamp (1902). Later, Susan B. Anthony would be the first American woman to appear on a coin – her dollar coin was minted from 1979-1981 until it was replaced by one featuring Sacajawea.)

Read More – *for Kids:* **Martha Washington** by Candice F Ransom, 2003. *for Teens and Adults:* **Martha Washington: An American Life** by Patricia Brady, 2006. **General and Mrs. Washington: The Untold Story of a Marriage and a Revolution** by Bruce Chadwick, 2006.

Visit: Mount Vernon VA (15 miles south of Washington DC) www.mountvernon.org
Morristown National Historical Park Morristown NJ www.nps.gov/morr/index.htm
Valley Forge National Historical Park King of Prussia, PA www.nps.gov/vafo/index.htm

Martha Washington (1731-1802) by Victoria Ford © 2016

"I little thought when the war was finished, that any circumstances could possibly have happened which would call the General into public life again. I had anticipated, that from this moment we should have been left to grow old in solitude and tranquility together... I am still determined to be cheerful and to be happy in whatever situation I may be, for I have also learnt from experience that the greater part of our happiness or misery depends upon our dispositions, and not upon our circumstances; we carry the seeds of the one, or the other about with us, in our minds, wherever we go."
– Martha Washington to Mercy Otis Warren, December 26, 1789

Dolley Madison (1768-1849) "Queen Dolley"
Masterful Behind-the-Scenes Politician

Dolley Madison was known for her fancy dresses and flamboyant hats, but underneath the plumage was a master politician. Dolley grew up in a Quaker family. After her father lost his business, Dolley's mother opened a boarding house in Philadelphia which prospered since the new Congress was meeting there. One day Senator Aaron Burr sent Dolley a message that an important man wanted to meet her. James Madison was seventeen years older than Dolley, tiny, shy and quiet but brilliant – he was known as the "Father of the Constitution." Dolley soon fell in love with "little Jimmy" (he was 5'4", she 5'6") and they were married in 1794. Since he was not a Quaker, Dolley was turned out of the Quaker Meeting – and happily ditched all her old dull clothing.

When Thomas Jefferson became president in 1801, he asked James Madison to become his Secretary of State. Jefferson's wife had died and, though he didn't approve of women in public life – he said they were *"too wise to wrinkle their foreheads with politics"* – Jefferson admired Dolley's skill at getting along with people. He asked her to help host events at the new President's House in Washington DC. Dolley excelled welcoming everyone – political friends and enemies, foreign ambassadors, even Indian chiefs – to the nation's new capital. Eight years later, when her husband ran for president, Dolley became his unofficial campaign manager. When he won, Dolley hosted an inaugural ball that was so crowded that windows were deliberately broken to let in air!

The new capital city was still under construction, and the place was muddy and miserable but Dolley set about making it a real center of government. Two months after moving in, she started "Mrs. Madison's Wednesday nights." Anyone could come to the President's House and practically everyone did – so many that the events came to be known as "squeezes." With food and music and laughter, these squeezes were fun, but they also became the place for people to make connections and help build their new country. Dolley was amazing. She never forgot a name or face and she was an expert people manager. If she heard men starting an argument, she would send over cake and punch. At dinners, she shocked everyone by sitting at the head of the table leading the conversation (so her shy husband didn't have to.) She was her husband's unofficial ambassador and spy – visiting every new Senator and Representative and taking groups of women to hear sessions in Congress and the Supreme Court. She read letters, newspapers, and listened to what people were saying – keeping her eyes and ears open for information which she passed on to her husband. When her husband's secretary was sick, she filled in. When her husband was sick, she attended events on behalf of the President. Dolley would say, *"You know I am not much of a politician"* then tell her husband what she thought about the subject – though she never took a stand in public.

"I am still here within the sound of the cannon!" Dolley wrote as the British invaded the city in 1814 while her husband was in Maryland inspecting the troops. Dolley jumped up from the dinner table, gathered important papers (and her parrot!) and instructed that the large portrait of George Washington be cut from its frame. Then, disguising herself as a farm woman, she bundled it all in a farm wagon and escaped, writing her sister *"I must leave this house or the retreating army will make me a prisoner in it by filling up the road I am directed to take."* Dolley's rescue of George Washington made her a national heroine – when the war ended, troops marched past her house giving three cheers in her honor!

For the rest of her life, people loved hearing stories from this bubbly woman who had known 12 presidents. One senator said she was *"the only permanent power in Washington."* She was given an honorary seat in Congress to watch debates and a lifetime of free postage. When she died, her funeral was so large it literally shut down Washington, and President Zachary Taylor called her "First Lady" – a title that has stuck ever since.

Read More – *for Kids:* **Dolley Madison: Parties Can Be Patriotic** (Women Who Broke the Rules) by Kathleen Krull, 2015. **The White House is burning** by Jane Sutcliffe, 2014, *for Teens & Adults:* **A Perfect Union: Dolly Madison and the Creation of the American Nation** by Catherine Allgor, 2006. DVD: **Dolley Madison: America's First Lady**. PBS, 2010

Visit: Montpelier Orange, VA www.montpelier.org/james-and-dolley-madison

Dolley Madison (1768-1849) "Queen Dolley" by Kim Huyler Defibaugh © 2016
Masterful Behind-the-Scenes Politician

Fascinating Factoid: British soldiers ate the dinner Dolley left behind before they set fire to the President's House, which then turned black on the outside from the smoke and fire damage. When the house was repaired and repainted white, it acquired its famous nickname, and in 1901, President Teddy Roosevelt officially named it the "White House." Today Dolley's portrait hangs in the Red Room at the White House and, when the door is open, it faces the portrait of George Washington that she saved.

Sacagawea (c 1790-1812?)
First Native American Woman Accorded the Right to Vote in an Official U.S. Government Venture

Sacagawea was born in the Shoshone tribe in the Rocky Mountains, then captured at around age 11 by the Hidatsa tribe during a bison hunt and taken to what is now North Dakota. A few years later she became the wife of French Canadian trapper Toussaint Charbonneau. They were living at a fort there in 1804 when Lewis and Clark's expedition stayed over the winter on their journey from the Missouri River to the Pacific Ocean. In April 1805, Sacagawea, her husband and their two-month-old son joined this expedition. She served as a negotiator and translator – the expedition wanted to trade for horses with the Shoshone in order to cross the Rocky Mountains. The Shoshone were wary of strangers but, by a stroke of luck, Sacagawea's brother was the Chief and the expedition got the horses they needed. Her gender also enabled peaceful interactions with other tribes, and her knowledge of botany helped the expedition find edible plants.

In November of 1805, the corps had almost reached the Pacific Ocean but needed to decide where to make winter camp. Each member had an equal say – and Sacagawea's vote counted alongside the others. After the journey was completed, Sacagawea and her family spent three years among the Hidatsa before accepting William Clark's invitation to move to St. Louis, Missouri in 1809. In 1812, William Clark became the foster father of Sacajawea's son and her infant daughter. There is some debate about what happened to Sacajawea, but most historians believe she died that year. Sacajawea's story lives on in paintings, statues, and the U.S. dollar coin.

Fascinating Factoid: Sacagawea's name came from the Hidatsa words for bird ("sacaga") and woman ("wea") but the Shoshone say that "Sacajawea" means boat-pusher in their language and is her real name. In North Dakota the official spelling is "Sakakawea." Some American Indian oral traditions relate that rather than dying in 1812, Sacagawea left her husband, Charbonneau, headed West and married into the Comanches, then returned to the Shoshone in Wyoming in 1860, where she died in 1884. This narrative was explored in University of Wyoming historian Grace Raymond Hebard's 1933 book **Sacajawea** and in the 1984 novel **Sacajawea** by Anna Lee Waldo.

Sarah Winnemucca (c1844-1891) was another Native American woman who later played a similar role. She spoke three native languages as well as Spanish and English and worked as interpreter and peacekeeper in the 1860s-70s between her people, the Paiute, and the U.S. Army and the Bureau of Indian Affairs (BIA). In 1878 she traveled alone over 100 miles to rescue her father who had been captured by the Bannock tribe and then spied on the tribe for the army which was then at war with the Bannocks. Sadly, her help was not repaid in kind. The Paiute were forced to move from their ancient lands to a reservation in Washington State. Winnemucca met with President Rutherford B. Hayes and his Secretary of the Interior in 1880. She was promised that they would have their own land, but corrupt BIA agents did not honor the promise. Sarah lectured widely, publicizing the sufferings and injustices done to her people, gathering signatures on a petition and telling their plight in her book **Life Among the Piutes**. Though she gathered hundreds of signatures, sold many copies and even got Congress to pass a bill ordering that the government give her tribe their own land, no one at BIA ever acted upon the law.

Read More (a sampling) *for Kids:* **Who Was Sacagawea?** by Judith Bloom Fradin, 2002. **Sacajawea: Lewis and Clarke Would Be Lost Without Me** by Kathleen Krull, 2015. *for Teens and Adults:* **Sacajawea** by Joseph Bruchac, 2008. She has also been featured in numerous films.

Visit: **Lewis and Clark National Historic** Trail ID, IL, IA, KS, MO, MT, NE, ND, OR, SD, WA www.nps.gov/lecl/index.htm.
There are more than 20 statues of Sacagawea around the country - a list is on her Wikipedia profile.
Place setting at Judy Chicago's *Dinner Party* **Brooklyn Museum**. www.brooklynmuseum.org/eascfa/dinner_party

Sacagawea by Diana Wilkoc Patton © 2016   www.dianapatton.com

*"The wife of Shabono our interpetr we find reconsiles all the Indians,
as to our friendly intentions a woman with a party of men is a token of peace."*– William Clark

Abolitionists and Suffragists:

- Phillis Wheatley (c.1753-1784) – Slave Poet and First African-American Woman Writer to be Published

- Margaret Fuller (1810-1850) Margaret Fuller (1810-1850) Author of *Woman in the Nineteenth Century,* a Founding Document of 19th Century Feminism.

- Frances (Fanny) Wright (1795-1852) – "The Most Shocking Woman in America" First Woman in America to Take a Public Stand Against Slavery and For Equal Opportunities for Women

- Maria W. Stewart (1803?-1879) – African American and Women's Rights Activist

- Sarah (1792-1873) and Angelina Grimke (1792-1873) – Abolitionists and Suffragists

- Lucretia Mott (1793-1880) – Abolitionist and Catalyst of the Seneca Falls Convention

- Elizabeth Cady Stanton (1815-1902) – Organizer of the Seneca Falls Convention and Author of the Declaration of Sentiments

- Amelia Bloomer (1818-1894) – Newspaper Editor, Promoter of the "Liberating" Outfit Named After Her

- Lucy Stone (1818-1893) – Suffragist and Orator, First Woman to Refuse to Give Up her Name Upon Marriage

- Susan B. Anthony (1820-1906) – Tireless Advocate for Women's Suffrage

- Matilda Joslyn Gage (1826 –1898) – Forgotten Suffragist

- Sojourner Truth (1797-1883) – Great Preacher and Abolitionist

- Harriet Tubman (c1820-1913) – "Moses of Her People" and "Queen of the Underground Railroad"

- Frances Ellen Watkins Harper (1825-1911) – Free-Born African-American Woman Who Lectured Widely on Abolition and Women's rights

- Esther Morris (1814-1902) – Wyoming Territory Women's Suffrage Advocate and First Woman Justice of the Peace

- Carrie Chapman Catt (1859-1947) – Leader of the National Woman Suffrage Association and Founder of the League of Women Voters

- Anna Howard Shaw (1847-1919) – Powerful Speaker for the Women's Suffrage Movement

- Harriot Stanton Blatch (1856-1940) – Working Class Suffrage Organizer

- Inez Milholland (1886 –1916) – "White Knight" and Martyr for the Women's Suffrage Movement

- Alice Paul (1885-1977) – Feminist, Suffragist, and Political Strategist

Phillis Wheatley (c.1753-1784)
Slave Poet and First African-American Woman Writer to be Published

A young African girl arrived on a slave ship in Boston in 1761. She was frail and trembling; she spoke no English and looked to be about seven years old. Susannah Wheatley bought the child to be her assistant with everyday tasks and gave her the first name "Phillis" (the name of the slave ship that had carried the girl to America) and their own last name of Wheatley, a common custom if a surname was used for slaves.

Susannah's husband, John Wheatley, was a Boston merchant and tailor and a well-known progressive thinker. The Wheatleys soon recognized that Phillis was very bright. They allowed her to be tutored by their daughter Mary and, within a year, Phillis could speak and read English fluently. Then their son tutored Phillis in Latin and the classics – an education unprecedented for a slave and highly unusual for a female. At the age of 14, she wrote her first poem, *To the University of Cambridge, in New England.* Recognizing her talent, the Wheatleys delegated the housework to other slaves, treated her like family and encouraged her to write and visit with influential people.

In 1767, Mrs. Wheatley had one of Phillis's poems published in a newspaper. Then, unable to find a book publisher in America for Phillis's poems, Mrs. Wheatley sent them to a publisher in England who said he would publish them only if she had proof they were written by an African girl. After signed statements from many of the best-known people in Boston were received, the book was published in London. In England, people could not believe that a young black slave was the author and were eager to meet her in person. So in 1773, Phillis herself went to London (accompanied by Nathaniel Wheatley), where she became quite a celebrity.

Phillis's poems gave abolitionists (opponents of slavery) proof that Africans were not dumb (something many slaveholders asserted) and that, if given education, they could be just as smart as whites. Ben Franklin, John Hancock, and George Washington were among Phillis's fans. Sadly, during the American Revolution, Mr. and Mrs. Wheatley both died. Phillis was freed in their wills, but though Phillis married and tried to support herself with poetry and sewing, she died nearly penniless in her early 30s.

Fascinating Factoid: In 1772, Phillis Wheatley legally defended her authorship of her poems in court. She was questioned by a group of Boston's literary, religious and political elites – including the governor of Massachusetts and John Hancock (whose large signature would later scroll across the Declaration of Independence – allegedly *"so King George could read it without his glasses."*) They concluded that she had written the poems and signed an attestation that was included as a preface to her book. In 1775, Phillis sent George Washington a poem she had dedicated to him and she later met with him. Some people think that meeting might have influenced his attitudes about slavery since his will instructed that his slaves be freed upon the death of his wife, Martha.

Read More – *for Kids:* **A Voice of Her Own: The Story of Phillis Wheatley, Slave Poet** by Kathryn Lasky, 2012. *For Teens and Adults:* **Women in Black History: Stories of Courage, Faith, and Resilience** by Tricia Williams Jackson, 2016. **Poems on Various Subjects, Religious and Moral** by Phillis Wheatley. **The Trials of Phillis Wheatley: America's First Black Poet and Her Encounters with the Founding Fathers** by Henry Louis Gates Jr., 2010.

Visit: Boston Women's Heritage Trail (Back Bay West Tour) bwht.org **Boston Women's Heritage Trail: Four Centuries of Boston Women: Guidebook, Walking Tours, and Maps.** Curious Traveler Press. 1999.

Phillis Wheatley by Diana Wilkoc Patton © 2016 www.dianapatton.com
Slave Poet and First African-American Woman Writer to be Published

"I, young in life, by seeming cruel fate
Was snatched from Afric's fancy'd happy seat:
What pangs excruciating must molest,
What sorrow labor in my parents' breast."

Margaret Fuller (1810-1850)
Author of *Woman in the Nineteenth Century*, a Founding Document of 19th Century Feminism

When Margaret was born in 1810, few options were available to women – they could be wives, mothers, teachers, prostitutes, factory workers, seamstresses, or slaves. Women were supposed to be quiet, docile and helpful – out of sight and out of mind – but Margaret would have none of that.

Margaret's father was a prominent lawyer-politician in Cambridge, Massachusetts. Disappointed that his first child was not a boy, he decided to give his daughter a rigorous education at home. He taught her to read and write when she was three, Latin at age five, then Greek, and soon she was translating the classics. After briefly attending a variety of schools for "Young Ladies," she returned home to Cambridge at age 16, teaching herself French, German and Italian and resuming her literary studies. When she was 19, her father lost his business and moved the family to an isolated farm in Groton. Margaret ended up running the household for her ailing mother and teaching and then helping to support her younger siblings after her father died when she was in her mid-twenties.

Despite crippling disabilities – a crooked spine, terrible migraines, painful nearsighted vision, and serious bouts of depression – Margaret set to work using her intellect, teaching and writing skills to advocate for social change as well as support her family. She taught school for two years in Providence then moved back to Boston in 1839 and began to host lectures and seminars in her house to earn money. Her lectures, called "Conversations" which both men and women attended, covered a variety of subjects including classics, mythology, fine arts, philosophy, health and women's rights. These provided a safe environment for women to engage their minds and discuss issues that were banned from polite society. She was a close friend of Ralph Waldo Emerson, Bronson Alcott, and Henry David Thoreau and a passionate supporter of the Transcendentalist movement which emphasized thoughtful individual self-reliance and nature – becoming the first editor of their philosophical magazine **The Dial** in 1840. There she wrote articles reviewing books and art and in 1843 published an essay *"The Great Lawsuit: Man versus Men, Woman versus Women "* advocating for women's political and economic rights. In 1845, she expanded it into the book **Woman in the Nineteenth Century** which laid the groundwork for feminist challenges to society's limits on women and had a major influence on the future leaders of the Women's Suffrage Movement in the United States, including Susan B. Anthony, Elizabeth Cady Stanton, and Lucretia Mott.

In 1844, publishing tycoon Horace Greenley hired Margaret to be America's first paid female literary critic at his paper **The New York Tribune.** While there, she became a strong advocate for American authors. Two years later, she sailed to Europe to become America's first female foreign correspondent. Initially reporting from Paris and London, she was regarded as a serious intellectual and met many prominent people. In 1847, she traveled to Rome where she fell in love with a young Italian nobleman. They married and she had a son in 1848 just as the Italian revolution was exploding around them. Inspired by the cause, she ran a soldier's hospital in Rome and began writing an eyewitness account of the revolution. After the Italian republic failed, Margaret and her family fled to Florence in 1849, then set sail for America the following year. Tragically, the ship ran aground in a storm off Fire Island, New York, and their bodies (and Margaret's manuscript) were never recovered. After her death her writings were published as **At Home and Abroad** (1856) and **Life Without and Life Within**(1858).

Fascinating Factoid: Margaret was the first woman permitted to use the library at Harvard College and had the reputation of being the best-read person in New England.

Read more – *for adults:* **Margaret Fuller: A New American Life** by Megan Marshall, 2013. **The Lives of Margaret Fuller: A Biography** by John Matteson, 2013. **Woman in the Nineteenth Century** by Margaret Fuller, 1845.

Margaret Fuller (1810-1850) by Victoria Ford © 2016

Pioneering Feminist, Courageous Journalist, Literary Critic & Writer

"We would have every arbitrary barrier thrown down. We would have every path laid open to women as freely as to men. If you ask me what offices they may fill, I reply — any."

Frances (Fanny) Wright (1795-1852) "The Most Shocking Woman in America"
First Woman in America to Take a Public Stand Against Slavery and For Equal Opportunities for Women

Born in Scotland to a wealthy family, Frances (Fanny) Wright was orphaned at age three but raised by an aunt who encouraged her to study the French Enlightenment thinkers. No dunce in the learning department, she wrote her first book at age 18. At age 23, excited by the writings of Jefferson and the idea of the American republic which was founded on the Enlightenment ideas she so admired, Frances sailed to America with her sister to see a play she had written be performed and see the country firsthand.

When she returned to Scotland, she published **Views of Society and Manners in America** (1821) which was widely read in Great Britain, the United States and across Europe. In 1821, she went to France to meet the Marquis de Lafayette, the Revolutionary War hero who had invited her there after reading some of her writings. She returned to the United States in 1824, accompanying Lafayette on a tour of the country, meeting and becoming friends with Thomas Jefferson, James Madison, and Andrew Jackson along the way. The following year, she became an American citizen and the first woman in America to take a public stand against slavery.

After discussing the idea with Lafayette and the former presidents, Fanny rode horseback to Tennessee, bought land and eleven slaves and established a model plantation/commune consisting of those slaves, along with free blacks and white workers. She planned to show that slaves could be educated and then earn their freedom and that the plantation would earn enough to purchase and thus free additional slaves. Frances named her experimental settlement Nashoba, the Chickasaw name for the Wolf River. She was only 30, she was rich and many people in Europe as well as the United States were excited by her ideas because she offered hope of a way to prepare slaves to be self-supporting citizens, while saving the South from the shock of the sudden loss of millions of dollars in investments.

Unfortunately she contracted malaria and, while she was in Europe recovering, rumors of inter-racial marriages on the plantation dashed financial support and her utopian community collapsed. No quitter, she tried another approach. She moved to another "new moral" community, New Harmony, Indiana. There on July 4th, 1828 she delivered her first lecture. Waving a copy of the Declaration of Independence, she insisted that men and women deserved the same basic human rights, equal opportunities for women and free public education for all children. Over the next few years, she lectured to packed houses of men and women across the country– breaking long-standing social conventions against women speaking in public. Newspapers and religious leaders called her a *"female monster"* and *"the most shocking woman in America."*

Seeking a wider audience for her message, she also became co-editor of the **New Harmony Gazette** (later called the **Free Enquirer** after it moved to New York City). In its pages, this free-thinker and social reformer continued to speak out against slavery but also advocated for better conditions for working people who were the victims of *"wage slavery."* She argued that women were men's equals and that true justice would only be achieved when *"the two persons in human kind–man and woman–shall exert equal influences in a state of equal independence."* Frances returned to Europe in the mid-1830s – but her writings from abroad continued to influence American reformers.

Fascinating Factoid: In the 1830s, admirers started "Fanny Wright" societies. Detractors used her name to ridicule women's rights advocates – calling them "Fanny Wrightists" (similar to being called a "Communist" in the 1950s).

Read More – *for Kids:* **Rabble Rousers: 20 Women Who Made a Difference** by Cheryl Harness, 2003. *for Teens and Adults:* **Fannie Wright: Rebel in America** by Celia Morris Eckhardt, 1992. **Reason, Religion, and Morals (Collected Lectures)** by Frances Wright.

Virtual Museum: germantownmuseum.org/ap14.php

Frances (Fanny) Wright (1795-1852) by Victoria Ford © 2016
"The Most Shocking Woman in America"

"The sight of slavery is revolting everywhere. But to inhale the impure breath of its pestilence in the free winds of America is odious beyond all that imagination can conceive."

Maria W. Stewart (1803?-1879) African American and Women's Rights Activist

First known American-born woman to publicly lecture to audiences that included both women and men and the first African-American woman to lecture about women's rights and make a public anti-slavery speech.

Maria, a free-born African American girl in Hartford, Connecticut, was orphaned at age five and became an indentured servant to a clergyman. Though she had no formal education beyond Sunday Sabbath schools, she educated herself by reading the books in the clergyman's library. Her indenture ended when she was 15, but Maria continued to support herself as a servant until 1826 when she married James Stewart, a Naval shipping agent who had been captured and taken as a prisoner of war by England during the War of 1812. Her marriage brought Maria into Boston's small free black middle class which was actively starting to advocate for abolition. Just three years later, James died and Maria learned first-hand how unfair laws were to women when the white executors of her husband's will revoked the inheritance he had left to her. Six months later, her mentor, African American abolitionist David Walker, was found dead outside his shop, and Maria became convinced that God was calling her to become a *"warrior...for God and for freedom"* and *"for the cause of oppressed Africa."*

When William Lloyd Garrison, the abolitionist publisher of **The Liberator** advertised for writings by black women, Maria brought him her essays on religion, racism and slavery. In 1831, he published her essay *Religion and the Pure Principles of Morality: the Sure Foundation on Which We Must Build* as a pamphlet. The following year, Maria began speaking out in public. Her first speech was to an all-female black audience at the African American Female Intelligence Society. In it, she used evidence from the Bible to defend her right to speak, talked about religion and justice and advocated activism for equal rights for women and blacks in much the way Sojourner Truth would two decades later. On September 21, 1832, Maria Stewart delivered a second lecture, this time to an audience that also included men – deeply shocking ("promiscuous") in the eyes of most ministers. The English-born Frances Wright had scandalized Americans by speaking in public in 1828 but Maria is considered the first American-born public lecturer (the Grimké sisters would follow in 1837). Her ideas were quite confrontational. Speaking at Franklin Hall before the New England Anti-Slavery Society, a mixed gathering of blacks and whites, she questioned whether free blacks were much more free than slaves, given the lack of opportunity and equality. She also questioned the plan to send free blacks back to Africa. This and other of her speeches and writings were printed in **The Liberator** in a section called the "Ladies Department." On February 27, 1833, Maria's third public lecture, *"African Rights and Liberty,"* caused an uproar when she stated that black men lacked *"ambition and requisite courage."* On September 21, 1833, she gave a fourth and final *"Farewell Address"* to Boston. Dismayed at the negative reaction toward her public speaking and her lack of impact, she ceased her speech-making, but in 1835, William Lloyd Garrison published all four speeches plus some essays and poems in **Productions of Mrs. Maria W. Stewart**, which may have inspired other women to begin public speaking on the cause.

Maria moved to New York and became a teacher and assistant principal and an advocate for literacy and for educational opportunities for African Americans and women. She attended the 1837 Women's Anti-slavery Convention and supported Frederick Douglass' newspaper, **The North Star**, but did not write for it. In the early 1850s, she moved to Baltimore and then to Washington, DC. in 1861. She continued to teach and in the 1870s also became head matron at the Freedman's Hospital and Asylum – a haven for former slaves who came to Washington – taking over the job previously held by Sojourner Truth. In 1878, she used her widow's pension from her husband's service in the War of 1812 to republish her **Meditations from the Pen of Mrs. Maria W. Stewart** with new material about her life during the Civil War. She died soon thereafter.

Read More – *for kids:* **Dinner at Aunt Connie's House** by Faith Ringgold, 1993. *for teens and adults:* **Maria W. Stewart, America's First Black Woman Political Writer: Essays and Speeches** edited by Marilyn Richardson, 1987. **Black Feminist Thought: Knowledge, Consciousness and the Politics of Empowerment** by Patricia Hill Collins, 1990. **Black Women in America: The Early Years, 1619-1899** edited by Darlene Clark Hine, 1993.

Visit: Boston African American National Historic Site Boston, MA www.nps.gov/boaf (Black Heritage Trail)
Museum of African American History Boston, MA maah.org/site14.htm

Maria W. Stewart (1803?-1879) by Victoria Ford © 2016
African American and Women's Rights Activist

"...shall I, for fear of feeble man who shall die, hold my peace?
Shall I for fear of scoffs and frowns, refrain my tongue? Ah, no!"
"Talk without effort is nothing."

Sarah (1792-1873) and Angelina Grimke (1805-1879) Abolitionists and Suffragists

Sarah and Angelina Grimke were the 6th and 14th children, respectively, born into an aristocratic slave-holding family in South Carolina. From an early age, Sarah recognized the cruelty of slavery. At age 12, she defied the law and taught her slave servant girl reading and writing. Then, frustrated at being denied the good education offered her brothers, she asked to be godmother to her newborn sister Angelina. Angelina absorbed her older sister's opinions on slavery along with her ABCs.

Sarah traveled to the North in 1818 to nurse her dying father and ended staying with some Quaker families after he died. Angelina joined her sister in Philadelphia in 1829, just as antislavery activism was growing. In 1835, Angelina wrote a letter to famed abolitionist William Lloyd Garrison who published it in his paper **The Liberator.** The following year, she published an **"Appeal to the Christian Women in the South"** urging Southern women not to stand idly by, but to use their moral influence and free any slaves they could. Sarah wrote a similar appeal **"Epistle to the Clergy of the Southern States."** The die was cast. The Grimke sisters were informed that if they ever returned to South Carolina they would be thrown in jail. They never went home again.

In 1836, Angelina and Sarah began traveling across New York and throughout New England giving anti-slavery talks sponsored by the American Anti-Slavery Society. Initially they gave "parlor-talks" limited to women but soon began talking to large crowds. They were among the first women to lecture in public – upsetting many people who believed women should be seen and not heard. Men booed and whistled. They were attacked both for their ideas and daring to voice them. A group of ministers called them *"unnatural women"* and warned of the dangers to a woman's character *"when she assumes the place and tone of a man as a public reformer."*

In 1838, Angelina received more criticism when she brought an anti-slavery petition with 20,000 signatures before the Massachusetts State Legislature and spoke out to the committee – the first woman ever to address a state legislature. These reactions convinced the sisters that they needed to work toward *"the breaking of every yoke"* – linking the idea of freedom for slaves with that of female equality and Sarah wrote **"Letters on the Equality of the Sexes and the Condition of Women"** one of the first declarations of the rights of women in America. These letters questioned existing laws that allowed husbands complete control over their wives, their wives' property and even their children. They also defended women's rights to speak out on moral issues *"whatever is right for a man to do is right for a woman to do."*

Fascinating Factoid: Harriet Beecher Stowe (1811-1896) would later wield another powerful pen. In 1852, her anti-slavery novel **Uncle Tom's Cabin** sold 300,000 copies. Its depiction of the horrors of slavery fueled many Northerners' determination to end the abominable institution. Southerners denounced the book as a lie. Upon meeting Harriet in 1862, Abraham Lincoln is reported to have said to her, *"So you're the little woman who wrote the book that started this big war."*

Read More – *for Kids:* **Sisters Against Slavery** by Stephanie Sammartino McPherson, 1995. *for Teens and Adults:* **The Grimké Sisters from South Carolina: Pioneers for Women's Rights and Abolition** by Gerda Lerner, 2004. *Historical fiction:* **The Invention of Wings** by Sue Monk Kidd, 2014.

Visit: americangirlsartclubinparis.wordpress.com/2015/05/01/the-invention-of-wings-the-grimke-sisters-in-charleston

"But perhaps you query, why appeal to women on this subject?
We do not make the laws which perpetuate slavery...I reply, I know you do not make the laws,
but I also know that you are the wives and mothers, the sisters and daughters of those who do;
and if you really suppose you can do nothing to overthrow slavery, you are greatly mistaken."
–Angelina Grimke (Appeal to the Christian Women of the South, 1836)

Sarah (1792-1873) and Angelina Grimke (1805-1879) Abolitionists and Suffragists by Kat Schroeder © 2016

"I believe it is a woman's right to have a voice in all the laws and regulations by which she is governed."
"...whatever is right for a man to do, is right for a woman to do."
– Sarah Grimke (Letters on the Equality of the Sexes, 1838)

Lucretia Mott (1793-1880) Abolitionist and Catalyst of the Seneca Falls Convention

Lucretia grew up in an unusually female-friendly environment for her time. She was born in Nantucket, Massachusetts, a town where women often managed businesses since so many of the men – including her own sea captain father – were away for months at a time on voyages. She was sent to a Quaker boarding school at age 13 and later became a teacher there. Her interest in women's rights was kindled when she discovered that similarly-qualified male teachers made three times her salary! When she was 18, Lucretia married James Mott, a fellow teacher and Quaker minister; she became a Quaker minister herself six years later. The Quakers were ardent abolitionists. Lucretia and James never wore cotton clothing or bought cane sugar or anything else produced on slave plantations. They made their home a stop on the Underground Railroad to assist slaves seeking their freedom and, with her husband's support, Lucretia traveled widely as a minister, giving sermons in support of abolition. In 1833, her husband helped found the American Anti-Slavery Society and she was the only woman allowed to speak at the convention. Frustrated at the Society's limits on women's participation, Lucretia, along with a group of white and black women, founded the Philadelphia Female Anti-Slavery Society. She became its first President and often preached at Black congregations. Their integrated organization soon aroused an angry response. During their 1838 Anti-Slavery Convention of American Women convention in Philadelphia, a mob destroyed Pennsylvania Hall where they were meeting and Lucretia and the white and black women delegates linked arms to escape the building!

In 1840, Lucretia and her husband attended the World's Anti-Slavery Convention in London and she was outraged that the female delegates were required to watch silently from the visitor's gallery. Lucretia discussed this humiliation with Elizabeth Cady Stanton, a young American she had met on the voyage over, and they realized they needed to fight for their own rights as well as those of African American slaves. It took eight years, but in 1848, on a visit to upstate New York, Lucretia and her sister met with Elizabeth and three other women. They decided to hold a convention in a church in Seneca Falls on July 19-20, 1848 to discuss the social, legal, and religious rights of women. To everyone's surprise, approximately 260 women and 40 men attended. Lucretia gave powerful speeches but she initially opposed Elizabeth's call for a women's right to vote, feeling it was too revolutionary an idea. For the next two decades, Lucretia and her husband traveled around the country lecturing on abolition, temperance, women's rights and world peace. Her fans called her speeches "psalms of peace." Detractors jeered and even threatened her with physical harm.

After the Civil War, Lucretia, already in her 70s, was elected the first president of the American Equal Rights Association, but resigned two years later. In 1869, Lucretia attempted to mend the split between Elizabeth Cady Stanton, Susan B. Anthony and Lucy Stone regarding the best strategy for the women's movement: suffrage for freedmen and all women, or suffrage for freedmen first. When she died in 1880, she was considered by many *"the greatest American woman of the 19th century."* She was a mentor and advisor to Elizabeth Cady Stanton, who continued to work for the cause for another two decades.

Fascinating Factoid: A new $10 bill to be released in 2020 (the 100th anniversary of the 19th Amendment granting women the right to vote) will feature Lucretia Mott, Sojourner Truth, Susan B. Anthony, Elizabeth Cady Stanton, and Alice Paul.

Read More – *for Kids:* **Lucretia Mott: A Photo-Illustrated Biography** by Lucille Davis, 1998. **Lucretia Mott: A Guiding Light (Women of Spirit)** by Jennifer Fisher Bryant, 1995. *for Teens and Adults:* **Lucretia Mott's Heresy: Abolition and Women's Rights in 19th-Century America** by Carol Faulkner, 2013.

Visit: Women's National Rights Historic Park, Seneca Falls, NY www.nps.gov/wori. **Lucretia Mott sculpture by Pablo Picasso** at the Carrier Dome, Syracuse. Lucretia, Elizabeth Cady Stanton and Susan B. Anthony are portrayed in a **sculpture by Adelaide Johnson** at the United States Capitol, which went on display in the crypt of the US Capitol in 1921 (the year after the 19th Amendment was passed). Since 1997, the sculpture has been on display in the rotunda.

Lucretia Mott (1793-1880) by B a r b a r a Schneider © 2016 . B a r b a r a Schneider @artavita.com
Abolitionist and Women's Rights Activist

"If our principles are right, why should we be cowards?"

"The world has never yet seen a truly great and virtuous nation, because in the degradation of women,
the very fountains of life are poisoned at their source."

Elizabeth Cady Stanton (1815-1902) – Women's Suffrage Pioneer
"We hold these truths to be self-evident: that all men AND WOMEN are created equal"

When Elizabeth was thirteen years old, she overheard a widow sobbing in her father's legal office – distraught that the family farm she had purchased with her own money would be going to her spendthrift son. Judge Cady explained that there was nothing he could do . The law said married women had no property rights – all that the woman owned, all that she earned, even her children were her husband's property and now her son's – she had no say in the matter. Elizabeth took a pair of scissors and cut the law from her father's legal books but Judge Cady explained to his daughter that it would do no good. Only men could change the laws because only men could vote. Elizabeth remained defiant. Twelve years later, when she married Henry Stanton in 1840, she refused to say "obey" in her vows.

Elizabeth Cady Stanton was traveling with her new husband to London for the World Anti-Slavery Convention when she met Lucretia Mott. Infuriated when the men wouldn't let them speak and relegated them to a separate curtained-off area in the balcony, they decided that women needed to advocate for their own rights. Between moves and three pregnancies, it took eight years but after a visit from Lucretia, a tired, lonely and frustrated Elizabeth decided to organize the world's first women's right's convention in her town of Seneca Falls, New York.

Elizabeth, Lucretia, and three other women put a notice in the local paper announcing a "women's rights convention" would be held on July 19-20, 1848. They were astonished when more than 300 people showed up. Elizabeth stood in front of an assembled company of men and women and opened the convention by reading aloud their official proclamation ***"The Declaration of Sentiments and Resolutions"*** – shocking many people who strongly believed that *"women should be seen not heard."* Modeled after the Declaration of Independence, her opening words differed by only two words *"and women"* but those words were considered radical indeed.

Elizabeth set off a raucous debate at the convention when she proposed that women be given the right to vote. Many women present (including Lucretia) thought this idea was too radical and that men would use it to shoot down all of the other proposals. Elizabeth argued that if women had the vote they could use it to obtain all the other things they were seeking. African American abolitionist Frederick Douglass took her side and gave a rousing speech on the universal right to vote. Her resolution passed by a small margin. Ultimately 68 women and 32 men signed the ***"Declaration of Sentiments"*** which outlined the wrongs done to women and demanded that all female citizens be given the right to vote. Elizabeth and many other advocates would spend the rest of their lives working toward that goal. Elizabeth even ran for Congress in 1866. She said that though she couldn't vote for men, men could vote for her!

Fascinating Factoid: Only one of the 100 people who signed the ***"Declaration of Sentiments"*** was still alive when the 19th Amendment granting women the right to vote became law 72 years later. Charlotte Woodward (1830-1921) was a nineteen-year-old glove maker when she heard about the convention and decided to go: *"At first we traveled quite alone...but before we had gone many miles we came on other waggon-loads of women, bound in the same direction. As we reached different cross-roads we saw waggons coming from every part of the country, and long before we reached Seneca Falls we were a procession."* Charlotte described her motivation, *"Every fibre of my being rebelled [against] all the hours that I sat and sewed gloves for a miserable pittance which, after it was earned, could never be mine."* She wanted the right *"to collect my wages."* Though Charlotte lived to see the 19th Amendment passed, sadly she was very ill and never got to cast her vote.

Read More – *for Kids:* **Elizabeth leads the way : Elizabeth Cady Stanton and the Right to Vote** by Tanya Lee Stone, 2008. **Elizabeth Started all the Trouble** by Doreen Rappaport, 2015. *for Teens and Adults:* **Elizabeth Cady Stanton : an American Life** by Lori D. Ginzberg, 2009. **Elizabeth Cady Stanton and Susan B. Anthony: a Friendship that Changed the World** by Penny Colman, 2011. **Eighty Years and More: Reminiscences 1815-1897** by Elizabeth Cady Stanton.

Visit: Women's National Rights Historic Park, Seneca Falls, NY www.nps.gov/wori

"THE BEST PROTECTION
ANY WOMAN CAN HAVE … IS COURAGE."

ELIZABETH CADY STANTON

Elizabeth Cady Stanton (1815-1902) by Mary Delaney Connelly © 2016

*"We do not expect our path will be strewn with the flowers of popular applause
but over the thorns of bigotry and prejudice will be our way."*

Amelia Bloomer (1818-1894)
Newspaper Editor and Promoter of the "Liberating" Outfit Named After Her

"We shall be allowed breathing-room and our forms shall be what nature made them."

In 1851, when Elizabeth Cady Stanton's cousin Libby Miller came for a visit to Seneca Falls, she wore a pair of ballooning trousers that hugged her ankles topped with a dress that only reached her knees. It was an outfit she had worn on her honeymoon in Switzerland to make hiking easier and now (with her husband's approval) had decided to wear every day. The people in town were shocked – women of the time were expected to wear heavy horsehair petticoats and a tight corset and *never* show their ankles. Elizabeth, however, delighted in the idea. She was eager to shed her "clothes prison" and quickly sewed herself a pair of black satin pants and a knee-length dress. Her father and eldest son protested, but Elizabeth was determined to continue wearing her new clothes. What was "immodest" about being able to carry both a baby and a candle without worrying about tripping and falling! And she relished being able to take deep breaths without having her lungs squeezed by a tight corset.

When Amelia Bloomer saw Elizabeth and Libby wearing the outfit, she decided she would wear it too. Amelia was a temperance (anti-alcohol) activist and in 1849 had been one of the founders of a temperance newspaper called *The Lily* – the first paper published, edited and typeset by women. Amelia thought that since women lecturers were considered "unseemly," writing was the best way for women to work for reform. Soon she became the sole editor and owner of the paper – broadening the content to include other areas of interest to women, including health and women's rights. After Amelia published a picture of herself in the new outfit, her office was flooded with requests for the patterns. Newspapers all over the country caricatured her and dubbed the new style "bloomers."

In the following years, *The Lily* published articles by Elizabeth advocating that women be allowed to vote and run for public office and it became one of the most influential publications dealing with women's issues in the country. Amelia, Elizabeth Cady Stanton and Susan B. Anthony wore bloomers on their lecture tours, shocking people not only by their clothing but by traveling without a male escort and by speaking out about women's rights. Men made cat-calls and called them "unladylike" for speaking in public, newspapers mocked them, some religious leaders called the outfit "devilish" and even many women thought their costume and their ideas most improper. Bloomers became the dress that symbolized women's demand for equal rights but, ironically, by 1859 the leaders of the movement stopped wearing them because they felt the uproar over the outfit distracted people from the message.

Fascinating Factoid: Suffragists abandoned bloomers on the lecture circuit but they (and other women) soon found another place to wear them – bicycling! Susan B. Anthony would remark, *" I stand and rejoice every time I see a woman ride by on a wheel ...I think [bicycling] has done more to emancipate women than anything else in the world."* Sue Macy tells how in **Wheels of Change: How Women Rode the Bicycle to Freedom (With a Few Flat Tires Along the Way).**

Read More – *for Kids:* **You Forgot Your Skirt, Amelia Bloomer! A Very Improper Story** by Shana Corey, 2000. **Bloomers!** by Rhoda Blumberg, 1993. *for Teens and Adults:* **Life and Writings of Amelia Bloomer** by DC Bloomer (Amelia's husband), 1895. Online resource: www.nps.gov/parkhistory/online_books/wori/shs4.htm

Visit: Women's National Rights Historic Park, Seneca Falls, NY www.nps.gov/wori

"Bloomerism – an American custom" John Leech Sketch from **Punch**, 1851.
The cartoonist was ridiculing the feminist "bloomer" by associating it with women smoking,
considered completely unfeminine during the Victorian period.

Amelia's own "Bloomerisms":

"Let men be compelled to wear our dress for awhile and we should soon hear them advocating a change."

"When you find a burden in belief or apparel, cast it off."

WOMAN'S EMANCIPATION.

(BEING A LETTER ADDRESSED TO MR. PUNCH, WITH A DRAWING, BY A STRONG-MINDED AMERICAN WOMAN.)

Harpers New Monthly Magazine, Aug. 1851

THE AGE OF BRASS.

or the triumphs of Woman's rights

42

A POSER FOR A BLOOMER.

Old Gentleman. "BEFORE I CAN ENTERTAIN YOUR PROPOSAL, AND GIVE MY CONSENT TO YOUR MARRYING MY SON, I MUST ASK YOU, WHETHER YOU ARE IN A POSITION—A—TO—A—KEEP HIM IN THE STYLE TO WHICH—A—I MAY SAY—HE HAS ALWAYS BEEN ACCUSTOMED? AHEM!"

No. VI.—SOMETHING MORE OF BLOOMERISM.

(BEHIND THE COUNTER THERE IS ONE OF THE "INFERIOR ANIMALS.")

No. V.—A PROBABLE INCIDENT IF BLOOMERISM ISN'T PUT DOWN.

Maid "IF YOU PLEASE, MISS, THE DRESSMAKER HAS BROUGHT HOME YOUR NEW—AHEM—FROCK."

No. VIII.—BLOOMERISM AT HOME.

Strong-minded Female. "NOW, DO PRAY, ALFRED, PUT DOWN THAT FOOLISH NOVEL, AND DO SOMETHING RATIONAL. GO, AND PLAY SOMETHING ON THE PIANO; YOU NEVER PRACTISE NOW YOU'RE MARRIED."

Lucy Stone (1818-1893)
Suffragist and Orator, First Woman to Refuse to Give Up her Name Upon Marriage

"She stirred the nation's heart on the subject of women's wrongs" – Elizabeth Cady Stanton

Growing up in Massachusetts, Lucy Stone was so infuriated when her father used Biblical passages to justify unequal treatment between his sons and daughters that she decided that she wanted to study Hebrew and Greek to determine if the Bible actually said those things. When her father refused to pay for her schooling, she worked as a teacher for nine years to earn the $70 tuition to go to Oberlin College – at the time the only co-educational college.

Lucy was an excellent student but declined the opportunity to write the commencement speech when she learned a male student would deliver it – Oberlin's rules prohibited a woman from speaking in a public gathering. Upset at this policy, Lucy and other women on campus formed a debate club that met in the woods. As Lucy stated, *"We shall leave this college with the reputation of a thorough collegiate course, yet not one of us has received any rhetorical or eloutionary training. Not one of us could state a question or argue it in successful debate."*

After graduating with honors in 1847 (the first Massachusetts woman to get a college degree), Lucy soon put her speaking skills to good use – traveling widely as a paid agent for the American Anti-Slavery Society. When her women's rights speeches created controversy within the Society, she began speaking on weekends on abolition and weekdays on women's rights. Her talks brought large crowds but also drew hostility – people tore down the posters advertising her talks, burned pepper in the auditoriums where she spoke, and pelted her with prayer books and other missiles.

In 1850, Lucy and Paulina Kellogg Wright Davis organized the first National Women's Rights Convention in Worcester, Massachusetts. It marked the beginning of an organized women's rights movement and, shockingly to many, called for *"Equality before the law without distinction of sex or color."* Susan B. Anthony attended and became an activist after hearing Lucy speak. At first Lucy, Susan, and Elizabeth Cady Stanton worked together. They rejoiced in the 13th amendment which abolished slavery, but the 15th amendment granting black males the right to vote split the movement. All three women had wanted it to include women, but Lucy supported it even when it didn't; Elizabeth and Susan refused. In 1869 Lucy and Julia Ward Howe (lyricist of *"The Battle Hymn of the Republic"*) left the National Woman Suffrage Association (NWSA) and founded the American Woman Suffrage Association (AWSA). Lucy then became the founder, funder, and editor of AWSA's **Woman's Journal** –*"the voice of the woman's movement."* While both groups had the same goal, they pursued different strategies – the AWSA worked to get women the vote state-by-state while NWSA sought a constitutional amendment and also worked on issues of concern to working-class women.

Fascinating Factoid: In 1855, when Lucy married Henry Blackwell (a fellow abolitionist and the brother of pioneer women doctors Elizabeth Blackwell and Emily Blackwell), they asked the minister to read a statement announcing that Lucy Stone would keep her own name because current marriage laws *"refuse to recognize the wife as an independent, rational being, while they confer on the husband an injurious and unnatural superiority"* Women who followed her example called themselves "Lucy Stoners."

Read more – *for Kids:* **With Courage and Cloth** by Ann Bausum, 2004. **Women Suffragists** by Diana Star Helmer, 1998. *for Teens and Adults:* **Lucy Stone: Pioneer of Women's Rights** by Alice Stone Blackwell *(Lucy's daughter),* 1930. **Lucy Stone: An Unapologetic Life** by Sally G. McMillen, 2015.

Visit: Oberlin, Ohio walking tour: www.oberlin.edu/external/EOG/LucyStonewalk-a-thonTour/LucyStoneTour.html **Women's Rights National Historical Park** Seneca Falls, NY www.nps.gov/wori/learn/historyculture/lucy-stone.htm

Lucy Stone (1818-1893) by B a r b a r a Schneider © 2016 . B a r b a r a Schneider @artavita.com

"I expect to plead not for the slave only, but for suffering humanity everywhere.
Especially do I mean to labor for the elevation of my sex." – Lucy Stone, 1847

Susan B. Anthony (1820-1906) Tireless Advocate for Women's Suffrage

Susan grew up in a Quaker family, committed to the cause of social justice – particularly the abolition of slavery and temperance (banning alcohol). As a teen, Susan sometimes helped out in her father's mill, where she saw that women often knew more about weaving than their male bosses yet were paid less. When she was 17, her father's business failed and her choices were two – marry or get a job. Seeing her sister trapped in an unhappy marriage with a controlling husband and no legal protections, Susan determined to stay single and become a teacher – though she bristled that as a woman she earned only a quarter of what a man would for the job.

In 1850, Susan heard abolitionist and woman's rights promoter Lucy Stone speak at the first National Woman's Rights Convention in Massachusetts. The following year, Amelia Bloomer introduced her to Elizabeth Cady Stanton. The two became great friends and powerful partners in the fight for equal rights for women. They were a study in contrasts. Susan was tall and slim – Elizabeth short and stout. Elizabeth was a great writer and full of ideas but needed to stay close to home because of her many children. Susan, unmarried, had the time and energy to travel and lecture widely. Elizabeth wrote the speeches; Susan rented the halls and took them on the road. Soon, whenever Susan wasn't traveling, she was staying with Elizabeth – helping around the house so Elizabeth could write. Elizabeth's husband remarked: *"Susan stirred the puddings, Elizabeth stirred up Susan, and then Susan stirs up the world!"*

For years they worked together with other men and women on anti-slavery and women's rights. However, in 1869, the 15th Amendment split the movements. It gave constitutional rights to all "citizens" but defined "citizen" as male – intentionally changing the wording of the Constitution to leave out women. When Susan and Elizabeth were called "selfish" by the president of the Anti-Slavery Society for protesting this wording, Elizabeth retorted, *"Do you believe the African race is composed entirely of males?"* Susan, Elizabeth, and Lucretia Mott then organized the new National Woman Suffrage Association to pursue a national strategy to get women the vote. Susan's lecture fees financed much of the organization. In 1878, the "Susan B. Anthony Amendment," guaranteeing a woman's right to vote in every state in the nation, was introduced in Congress – but passage would take another 42 years! Neither Elizabeth (who died in 1902) nor Susan (who died in 1906) would live to see it become the 19th Amendment to the Constitution 72 years after Seneca Falls.

Fascinating Factoid: Susan was not afraid to wrestle with the law in court. In 1868, Susan and Elizabeth started a magazine called ***The Revolution*** with the motto *"Men, their rights and nothing more: women, their rights and nothing less."* When asked to pay taxes on the profits from ***The Revolution,*** Susan refused on the grounds that it was *"taxation without representation."* Then in 1872, Susan and nearly fifty other women in Rochester attempted to vote for Ulysses S. Grant in the presidential election. Susan was arrested and while awaiting trial, she lectured widely, asking her audiences *"Is it a Crime for a U.S. Citizen to Vote?"* Saying that the 14th Amendment gave her that right, she proclaimed, *"We no longer petition legislature or Congress to give us the right to vote, but appeal to women everywhere to exercise their too long neglected 'citizen's right.'"* The case garnered national publicity. After the judge sentenced her to pay a fine of $100, she responded, *"I shall never pay a dollar of your unjust penalty"* – and she never did. Susan was not jailed for not paying because the judge did not want her case to go to the Supreme Court. However when another case on women's voting rights reached the Supreme Court two years later, the justices ruled that the 14th Amendment did not give women the right to vote and that states were free to make their own voting rules. Ironically, Southern states soon used that ruling to create poll taxes and literacy tests to deter or eliminate African American men from voting.

Read More (a sampling) *for Kids:* **Heart on Fire: Susan B. Anthony Votes for President** by Ann Malaspina, 2012. **Marching with Aunt Susan** by Claire Rudolf Murphy, 2011. **Susan B. Anthony** by Alexandra Wallner, 2012. **Friends for Freedom: The Story of Susan B. Anthony and Frederick Douglass** by Suzanne Slade, 2014. **Who Was Susan B. Anthony?** by Pam Pollack, 2014. *for Teens and Adults:* **Not for Ourselves Alone: the Story of Elizabeth Cady Stanton and Susan B. Anthony** by Geoffrey C. Ward, 1999 (also a DVD).

Visit: **Susan B. Anthony Museum and House**, Rochester NY   www.susanbanthonyhouse.org
Women's National Rights Historic Park, Seneca Falls, NY www.nps.gov/wori
Place setting at Judy Chicago's *Dinner Party* **Brooklyn Museum**. www.brooklynmuseum.org/eascfa/dinner_party

Susan B. Anthony (1820-1906) Tireless Advocate for Women's Suffrage by Monisha Kulkarni © 2016

"There is not one foot of advance ground upon which women stand today that has not been obtained through the hard-fought battles of other women." – Susan B. Anthony, 1897

Matilda Joslyn Gage (1826 –1898) – Forgotten Suffragist

Matilda grew up in Cicero, New York, the only child of the only doctor in town. Both her parents encouraged her to read, learn, think, question and act on her beliefs. They were active abolitionists and her home was a station on the Underground Railroad. She, herself, would later risk prison and a $2000 fine after the Fugitive Slave Law of 1850 criminalized assistance to escaped slaves. Matilda had big dreams – she wanted to become a doctor. Her father had given her an extraordinary education: art, music, literature, Greek, philosophy, mathematics, plus the anatomy and physiology a doctor would need to know. But when she applied for admission at Geneva Medical College, her application was refused – no women were allowed. Instead 18-year-old Matilda married and was soon a mother. Because she had young children to care for, Matilda missed the 1848 Seneca Falls Women's Rights Convention and the one in 1850. But in 1852, when she was 26 years old, she attended the National Women's Rights Convention in Syracuse, New York. There she met Susan B. Anthony and made her first speech ever – in front of 2000 people! It was a remarkable speech. Showing both an amazing intellect and a sympathy for the poor and abused women in society, she quoted Goethe and Sir Isaac Newton, pointed out many examples of extraordinary women in history, then showed how the plight of poor and working women was a result of the unfair laws society imposed upon them. She soon became an active speaker and writer for the movement.

In 1869, she joined Susan B. Anthony and Elizabeth Cady Stanton to create the new National Woman Suffrage Association (NWSA) and was an officer for over 20 years. She and nine other women attempted to vote in 1871 and she made compelling legal and moral arguments in 21 speeches defending Susan B. Anthony's right to vote after Susan was put on trial for trying to cast a ballot for Victoria Woodhull in the 1872 presidential election. Matilda worked hard to get the right to vote in New York and in 1880, after New York granted women the right to vote in school elections, Matilda led 102 other women to the polls. Along with Susan B. Anthony and Elizabeth B. Stanton, she wrote and edited the first three volumes of **The History of Woman Suffrage**.

However in 1890, Susan B. Anthony, seeking a stronger united voice for women's suffrage, spearheaded the merger between NWSA and the American Woman Suffrage Association (AWSA). AWSA members supported the suffrage movement because they believed women's votes would achieve temperance and Christian political goals. Matilda and Elizabeth Cady Stanton felt that this violated the separation of church and state. After the merger, Matilda founded the Woman's National Liberal Union (WNLU) as a place for radical and liberal women's rights activists and became its president and the editor of its official journal, *The Liberal Thinker.* In 1893, Matilda published the book **Woman, Church and State** arguing that Christianity had oppressed women and reinforced patriarchal systems and that religion had no place in government. Her book also decried the brutal treatment of Native Americans and praised the Haudenosaunee (Iroquois) society which was a 'Matriarchate' in which women had true power, noting that descent through the female line and female property rights led to a more equal relationship between men and women. (Matilda had lived among the Haudenosaunee and been given the name Karonienhawi "she who holds the sky" when she was initiated into the Wolf Clan and the Council of Matrons – the tribal elder females who chose the chiefs.) Matilda died in 1898, a few months before the 50th anniversary of the first woman's rights convention. Her memorial stone reads, *"There is a word sweeter than Mother, Home or Heaven. That word is Liberty."*

Fascinating Factoids: Matilda's youngest daughter married L. Frank Baum, the creator of **The Wizard of OZ** stories and Matilda was the inspiration for the good witch Glenda. Ironically, Matilda was literally written out of the history of the suffrage movement. Susan B. Anthony, who outlived Matilda, chose her own biographer, Ida Hustad Harper, to write the 4th volume of the **History of Women's Suffrage 1883-1900** and Ida eliminated any mention of Matilda's contributions. In 1993, the scientific historian Margaret W. Rossiter created the term "Matilda effect" to describe when female scientists receive less credit for their scientific work than it deserves.

Read More – *for kids:* **Matilda Joslyn Gage** by Darlene Beck Jacobson *(forthcoming), for teens and adults:* **Sisters in Spirit** by Sally Roesch Wagner, 2001. **Matilda Joslyn Gage: She Who Holds the Sky** 1998. **Excluded from Suffrage History: Matilda Joslyn Gage, Nineteenth-Century American Feminist** by Leila R. Brammer, 2000.

Visit: The Matilda Joslyn Gage Foundation Fayetteville, NY www.matildajoslyngage.org

Matilda Joslyn Gage (1826 –1898) – Forgotten Suffragist by Victoria Ford © 2016

In 1878 Matilda bought the **Ballot Box**, a small monthly journal of a Toledo, Ohio suffrage association and transformed it into **The National Citizen and Ballot Box.** Under the banner *"The Pen Is Mightier Than The Sword,"* she included regular columns about prominent women in history and female inventors. Her goal was *"to secure national protection to women citizens in the exercise of their rights to vote"* but also to *"oppose Class Legislation of whatever form...Women of every class, condition, rank and name will find this paper their friend."* She was a witty and shrewd writer. Noting that laws allowed a man to give his children to a guardian unrelated to their mother in his will, she remarked, *"It is sometimes better to be a dead man than a live woman."*

Sojourner Truth (1797?-1883)
Abolitionist and Women's Rights Advocate

Isabella Baumtree (her slave name) was a two-year-old slave in New York State when the state passed a law ordering that slaves be freed – but not till July 4, 1827, when she would be about 30! So Isabella grew up in slavery, was sold four times and regularly abused. After her last owner broke his promise to free her a year early if she worked extra hard, Isabella ran away with her baby, but she had to leave her other children behind. The following year, she learned that her five-year-old son, Peter, had been sold South rather than freed as the law ordered. Furious, she sought the help of Quaker lawyer , fought in court and won, recovering her son who had been badly beaten. It was one of the first cases in which a black woman succeeded in winning a case against a white man in an American court.

Isabella moved to New York City and found work as a maid and a cook. On June 1, 1843, she had a vision telling her to become a traveling preacher. She gave herself a new name – Sojourner (traveler). She soon added a second name – Truth *"The Lord gave me Truth because I was to declare the truth to the people."* Leaving her home with a quarter and a new dress, she walked alone through Long Island, New York, and Connecticut, stopping at churches, camp meetings, and street corners to preach God's love. In Massachusetts, she met Frederick Douglass, another ex-slave and great abolitionist speaker. They became great friends and she started speaking out against slavery as well. Tall and slim, with *"the air of a Queen"* she won many converts to the anti-slavery movement with her deep, strong voice. In 1850, she published **The Narrative of Sojourner Truth.** It told her life story but was not written by her since, like most slaves, she had never learned to read or write. That same year, she became active in the women's rights movement and was a frequent but controversial speaker at Women's Rights Conventions. Opponents – and even some women's rights supporters – thought it most improper that a black woman would speak in public. She was often heckled and sometimes beaten. In 1851, when a group of clergymen started taunting the speakers at a women's rights convention in Ohio, she responded with one of the most famous speeches in American history: *"The man over there says women need to be helped into carriages and lifted over ditches... Nobody ever helps me into carriage...I could work as much and eat as much as a man – when I could get it – and bear the lash as well! And ain't I a woman..."*

Though a pacifist, she realized that the Civil War might be the only way to end slavery and encouraged blacks to join the Union Army. In 1864, upset that escaped slaves fleeing to Washington D.C. were living in muddy tent camps, she met with President Lincoln to try to get them food, housing, and job training. After the war, she traveled across the country speaking in her powerful, deep voice about freedom and human rights. A Detroit newspaper described her as having *"a heart of gold"* and *"a tongue of flame."* She talked to lawmakers arguing that the United States government owed slaves land and money to make up for the years it had allowed slavery to exist but, though some government officials agreed with her plan, it did not pass. She also spoke at women's rights gatherings – often the only black and the only poor woman in attendance. She argued that voting was important but that better wages for women were critical as well. Believing women needed to act, she attempted to vote in the 1872 election but her vote was blocked.

Fascinating Factoids: Nearly 100 years before Rosa Parks, Sojourner Truth rode horse-drawn streetcars in Washington, DC to demonstrate that black passengers should be allowed to sit next to whites. On July 4,1997 – 200 years after her birth – NASA's Mars rover Sojourner (named in her honor) landed on the red planet.

Read More – *for Kids:* **My Name is Truth: The Life of Sojourner Truth** by Ann Turner, 2015. **Sojourner Truth's Step-Stomp Stride** by Andrea Davis Pinkney, 2009. **Who Was Sojourner Truth?** by Yona Zeldis McDonough, 2015. *for Teens and Adults:* **The Narrative of Sojourner Truth** by Sojourner Truth and Olive Gilbert, 1850.

Place setting at Judy Chicago's *Dinner Party* **Brooklyn Museum.** www.brooklynmuseum.org/eascfa/dinner_party
Visit: Sojourner Truth Institute Battle Creek MI www.sojournertruth.org
Sojourner Truth Memorial Florence, MA sojournertruthmemorial.org (African-American Heritage Walking Tour)

Sojourner Truth (1797?-1883) by Jill Obrig © 2016

*"There is a great stir about colored men getting their rights but not a word about the colored women theirs.
You'll see, the colored men will be masters over the women."*

*"I am glad to see that men are getting their rights, but I want women to get theirs,
and while the water is stirring, I will step into the pool."*

Harriet Tubman (c1820-1913)
"Moses of Her People" and "Queen of the Underground Railroad"

Harriet's parents were warriors in West Africa, stolen from the Ashanti tribe in West Africa and sold as slaves in America. Growing up, Harriet worked as a field slave and received frequent whippings which left permanent scars on her back. Even worse, at age 13, an overseer threw a weight that hit her in the head, crushing part of her skull. As a result, she would experience sudden blackouts for the rest of her life. She married John Tubman, a free black man, but she was still a slave and could be sold at any time. A white neighbor told her about the "Underground Railroad," a secret network of people – free blacks and whites – who would help runaway slaves escape to freedom in the North and in 1849 29-year-old Harriet decided she would escape. Her husband, fearing she would be captured, refused to go – so Harriet fled alone. She traveled through the dark night to a safe house and received occasional rides hidden in wagons, but mostly walked 100 miles along back roads and forest paths by night until she reached free Philadelphia and got a job in a hotel kitchen.

She was safe – but what about her family? In 1850, Harriet did the unthinkable. She decided to return to Maryland to help them escape – even though doing so meant she risked capture as a runaway slave. Between 1850-1860, Harriet would make at least 13 dangerous trips and bring anywhere from 70 to 300 slaves (sources vary) north to freedom, including her aged parents. She was a strict leader by necessity. No one was allowed to turn back because they might be forced to give away the secrets of the people running the Underground Railroad. Harriet was clever – once when slave hunters were on her trail, she went south rather than north until the danger was past. She also spoke out publicly, telling white audiences about the horrors of slavery.

With the outbreak of the Civil War in April 1861, Harriet became a nurse, cook, scout and spy for the Union Army, often going behind the enemy lines in the South, talking with the slaves and gleaning important information about Confederate soldiers and supplies. As an Army scout, she was the first woman to lead an armed expedition during the war– bringing 150 African American soldiers on a raid to destroy Confederate supplies and free more than 700 slaves. However, the Army paid Harriet no salary so she baked and sold pies and gingerbread and brewed root beer to support herself.

Fascinating Factoid: After the war, Harriet returned to her home in Auburn NY but faced foreclosure because the government offered her no pension. Her neighbor, Sarah Bradford, offered to help write her story (Harriet was illiterate). Published in 1869, it became very popular, and Harriet was able to keep her house. The following year, she married a black soldier she had met when she was an Army guide in South Carolina and 30 years after the end of the war, the army finally gave Harriet $20 a month – her husband's pension! She used it to build a larger house next door "The Harriet Tubman Home for the Aged" to care for impoverished elderly African Americans. Ironically, she lost her money in a swindle and wound up living there herself. In her later years, Harriet became an activist for women's rights. She told a visitor, *"Tell the women to stand together"* a month before her death at age 93. She was buried with full military honors.

Read More *for Kids:* (a sampling) **Moses: When Harriet Tubman Led Her People to Freedom** by Carole Boston Weatherford (Caldecott Honor Book illustrated by Kadir Nelson), 2006. **Who Was Harriet Tubman?** by Yona Zeldis McDonough, 2002. **Aunt Harriet's Underground Railroad in the Sky** by Faith Ringgold, 1992. *for Teens and Adults:* **Harriet Tubman: The Moses of Her People** by Sarah Bradford, 1869. **Harriet Tubman: The Road to Freedom** by Catherine Clinton, 2004.

Visit: Harriet Tubman Underground Railroad Byway Eastern Shore, MD harriettubmanbyway.org
Harriet Tubman Underground Railroad National Historic Park Cambridge MD www.nps.gov/hatu
Smithsonian National Museum of African American History and Culture Washington DC nmaahc.si.edu

Harriet Tubman (c1820-1913) "Moses of Her People" by Jasmine R. Florentine © 2016   jasmineflorentine.com

"I think slavery is the next thing to hell."

*"I had reasoned this out in my mind. There was one of two things I had a right to – liberty or death.
If I could not have one, I would have the other."*

Frances Ellen Watkins Harper (1825-1911)
Free-born African-American Woman, Poet and Novelist who Lectured Widely on Abolition and Women's Rights

"I could not rest if I heard the tread
Of a coffle gang to the shambles led
And the mother's shriek of wild despair
Rise like a curse on the trembling air."

Free-born in Baltimore, Maryland, Frances worked as a maid and seamstress. In 1845, at age 20, she published her first book of poems and in 1854, her second book of poetry sold 12,000 copies! That same year, Frances gave a speech in New Hampshire titled "Education and the Elevation of the Colored Race."

In 1851, alongside William Still, chairman of the Pennsylvania Abolition Society, she helped escaped slaves along the Underground Railroad on their way to Canada. She began her career as a public speaker and political activist after joining the American Anti-Slavery Society in 1853. She lectured widely around the eastern U.S. on abolition and women's rights. When slavery was abolished after the Civil War, she focused her lectures on advocating for equal educational opportunities for women and African Americans.

In 1866, men and women abolitionists formed the American Equal Rights Association to work toward voting rights for both women and African Americans. Soon, however, conflict erupted. The Republican Party proposed the 15th amendment, giving voting rights for black men but not for women. Elizabeth Cady Stanton remarked that an educated female voter was better than an uneducated black or immigrant voter. Frederick Douglass, who had been a supporter of women's rights, countered, *"When women, because they are women, are hunted down...they will have an urgency to obtain the ballot equal to our own."* Bitter debate divided the suffrage movement. Frances and Lucy Stone supported Frederick Douglass. Sojourner Truth, Elizabeth Cady Stanton, and Susan B. Anthony insisted that women and African Americans should gain the vote at the same time. The 15th Amendment granting voting rights only to black men won out. It would take thousands of courageous and tenacious women 50 more years to get the 19th Amendment passed, granting women that same right.

In 1894 Frances helped found the National Association of Colored Women and served as its vice president. She died in 1911, nine years before women gained the right to vote.

Fascinating Factoid: In 1892, at age 67, Frances published a novel called **Iola Leroy** – the first novel published by an African American woman.

Read More – *for Kids and Teens: :* **Women in Black History: Stories of Courage, Faith, and Resilience** by Tricia Williams Jackson, 2016. *for Adults:* **A Brighter Coming Day: A Frances Ellen Watkins Harper Reader** by Frances Smith Foster. **Poems** by Frances Smith Foster. **Iola Leroy or Shadows Uplifted** by Frances E. W. Harper. **Discarded Legacy: Politics and Poetics in the Life of Frances E. W. Harper, 1825-1911** by Melba Joyce Boyd, 1994. **A People's History of the United States** by Howard Zinn.

Visit: Smithsonian National Museum of African American History and Culture Washington DC nmaahc.si.edu

"It is said that the Negro is ignorant. But why is he ignorant?
It comes with ill grace from a man who has put out my eyes to make a parade of my blindness–to reproach me for my poverty when he has wronged me of my money.... If he is poor, what has become of the money he has been earning for the last two hundred and fifty years? Years ago it was said cotton fights and cotton conquers for American slavery. The Negro helped build up that great cotton power in the South, and in the North his sigh was in the whir of its machinery, and his blood and tears upon the warp and woof of its manufactures."

Frances Ellen Watkins Harper (1825-1911) by Kim Wood © 2016   kimwoodstudio.com
Free-born African-American woman, poet and novelist who lectured widely on abolition and women's rights

"So close is the bond between man and woman that you cannot raise one without lifting the other.
The world cannot move ahead without woman's sharing in the movement,
and to help give a right impetus to that movement is woman's highest privilege."

Esther Morris (1814-1902)
Wyoming Territory Women's Suffrage Advocate and First Woman Justice of the Peace

Wyoming can claim many firsts for women: the right to vote, the first woman governor, and the first woman judge in American history, Esther Hobart Morris.

Born in New York State and orphaned at a young age, Esther showed she was an enterprising woman from the start. After an apprenticeship with a seamstress, she started her own hat shop and was a successful businesswoman by her early twenties. As a young woman, Esther was active in women's societies working to abolish slavery. She married at age 26. Just three years later, her husband died and she was left with an infant son. She soon remarried and had two more sons. The family moved to Illinois in 1845 because Esther wanted to claim her late husband's estate. Once there, she was informed that it would be impossible – Illinois law made it illegal for women to own or inherit property. In the spring of 1868, Esther's husband and her eldest son moved to the newly created Wyoming Territory to open a saloon to serve the booming gold mining town. The following year, Esther and her other sons joined them. Conditions in their small cabin were not for the faint of heart – high winds, brutally-cold temperatures and snow that could last until June.

At the time, the women's suffrage movement in the East had stalled. The 15th Amendment giving black men the right to vote had split the movement, and there was disagreement about what tactics to use next. In addition, many men feared that women would refuse to fulfill their domestic roles if granted equal rights. Some stories say that Esther invited candidates in Wyoming's 1869 election to tea and then had each man promise that if he won, he would support a law allowing women to vote – arguing that if women voted, it would bring law and order and morality to what was then a very Wild Western frontier territory. What is known is that in November 1869, William Bright, a saloon owner and territorial representative who was eager to promote the Wyoming Territory and to attract more women settlers, introduced a bill giving women the right to vote and hold public office – and the all-male Territorial Legislature passed it.

In December 1869, the Governor signed the first bill in the nation giving women the right to vote: *"Every woman of the age of twenty-one years, residing in this Territory, may at every election to beholden under the law thereof, cast her vote."* Informed of the new law, Susan B. Anthony urged Eastern women to migrate en masse to the State. Two months later, the Governor asked Esther to become Justice of the Peace, ironically, to serve out the term of a man who had resigned in protest after the women's suffrage amendment passed. In this rough and tumble mountain community where men outnumbered women 4 to 1, Judge Esther Morris tried miners, gamblers, brawlers, idlers and drunks – including her own husband whom she had arrested for assault and battery. Despite having little formal education, she had good legal sense. None of the 70 cases she tried was overturned. One of the lawyers who practiced before her recalled that *"to pettifoggers [dubious lawyers] she showed no mercy."*

Fascinating Factoid: In 1869, women in Wyoming had the most rights in the country – the territory's constitution gave women the right to vote and married women the right to own property, sign contracts, sue in court and serve on juries. The territory also gave all public employees (including teachers) equal pay for the same work – more than a century before that idea would gain traction in the country as a whole. When Wyoming applied for statehood in 1890, Congress asked that it restrict women's voting rights, but the legislature refused and Wyoming women became the only women in the country who could vote in Federal elections. Colorado's women won that right in 1893, Utah and Idaho gave their women the vote in 1896.

Read More – *for Kids:* **I Could Do That! : Esther Morris Gets Women the Vote** by Linda White, 2005. **When Esther Morris Headed West: Women, Wyoming, and the Right to Vote** by Connie Nordhielm Wooldridge, 2001.

Visit: Morris Monument Wyoming State Capitol Building Cheyenne, WY, replica in Capitol Rotunda, Washington D.C. **Wyoming State Museum** wyomuseum.state.wy.us

Esther Morris (1814-1902) by Arlene Holmes © 2016
First Woman Justice of the Peace and Suffrage Advocate

Carrie Chapman Catt (1859-1947) – Tireless Activist for Women's Suffrage
Leader of the National Woman Suffrage Association and Founder of the League of Women Voters

Carrie spent her childhood on the Western frontier and was an independent free-thinker from an early age – she asked her mother why she wasn't going to town with her father to vote! Carrie taught school to earn money for college at Iowa State and, once there, demanded to speak at the Crescent Literary Society, something only men were permitted to do. When the society finally granted her permission, she organized a debate on women and the vote. By the time she graduated in 1880, she was an articulate spokeswoman on the topic. After the sudden death of her young husband, she began organizing women's suffrage clubs and, in 1890, became Iowa's delegate at the first newly-merged National American Woman Suffrage Association (NAWSA) convention where she met Susan B. Anthony, Elizabeth Cady Stanton and Lucy Stone. Soon after the convention, she met and married her second husband – but was so passionate about suffrage that she required him to sign an agreement that she could work for suffrage four months of the year before she would accept his offer of marriage.

Carrie's imagination, drive and organizational talents quickly got the attention of the leaders of the NAWSA. In 1892, she addressed Congress asking for a women's suffrage amendment but she spent most of her time working tirelessly organizing women state-by-state. It was slow work – by 1896, only four states (Wyoming, Colorado, Utah, and Idaho) had granted women the vote and it would take 15 years to get another. In 1900, Susan B. Anthony retired as President of NAWSA and asked Carrie to take her place. In just a few years, Carrie refashioned NAWSA into a much more efficient organization as well as working to create an International Women's Suffrage Alliance. Carrie left the NAWSA presidency in 1904 to nurse her husband and was succeeded by Dr. Anna Howard Shaw. However, the group was weakened when a radical contingent led by Alice Paul split off. When Carrie was re-elected NAWSA President in 1915, she re-energized it – hiring a board of directors and setting up a group to lobby Congress, all as part of her "Winning Plan." It was a two step approach: getting state legislatures to give women the vote and then using the new female voting power to pressure Congress to pass a federal amendment. American women enthusiastically embraced her plan – membership jumped from 100,000 in 1915 to 2,000,000 in 1917.

Though she was a pacifist and had co-founded the Women's Peace Party, she also made a strategic decision when the U.S. entered the war in 1917. She became a member of President Wilson's Commission on Women and National Defense – actively encouraging women to support the war effort to impress voters with their patriotism. She still pursued her *"red-hot-never-ceasing campaign"* to get women the vote. In 1915, seven more states granted women's suffrage, by 1918 four more. Finally in June 1919, due to the combined efforts of Alice Paul's campaign and the strategies of NAWSA, the 19th Amendment, granting all women citizens of the U.S. the right to vote, passed Congress, Carrie campaigned for 14 months to get 36 states to ratify it and, on August 26, 1920, the 19th Amendment was incorporated into the Constitution. Shortly before women won the vote, Carrie founded the League of Women Voters because she felt women voters should be educated voters. She wrote *"The vote has been costly. Prize it."*

Fascinating Factoid: The first woman to vote might have been Stagecoach driver Charley Parkhurst who is said to have voted in the 1868 California presidential election. When "he" died a few years later, it was discovered that "he" was Charlotte Parkhurst. Her tale is told in **Rough Tough Charley** by Verna Kay, 2007 and the novel **Charley's Choice: The Life and Times of Charley Parkhurst** by Fern J Hill, 2012. Another colorful driver was "Stagecoach Mary." Mary Fields was the first African American woman to work for the U.S. Postal Service. In her sixties, she drove the route with horses and a mule and her reliability earned her the nickname "Stagecoach." When the snow was too deep for her horses, she strapped on snowshoes, and delivered the mail carrying the sacks on her shoulders. Her character has appeared in several movie and television shows and her story is told in the book **More than Petticoats: Remarkable Montana Women** by Gayle Shirley, 2011.

Read More – *for Teens and Adults:* **Votes for Women! The Story of Carrie Chapman Catt** by Barbara A. Somervill, 2003. DVD: **One Woman, One Vote**. PBS, 2006.

Visit: Belmont-Paul Women's Equality National Monument Washington, DC
nationalwomansparty.org/learn/womens-history-in-the-u-s

Carrie Chapman Catt (1859-1947)

by Laura Leigh Myers
© 2016

Leader of the National Woman Suffrage Association and Founder of the League of Women Voters

"How is it possible that woman who is unfit to vote, should be the mother of, and bring up, a man who is?"

"Roll up your sleeves, set your mind to making history and wage such a fight for liberty that the whole world will respect our sex." – Nov. 1915, calling women to try yet again for women's suffrage in New York after a referendum defeat.

Anna Howard Shaw (1847-1919)   Powerful Speaker for the Women's Suffrage Movement

Anna's lonely childhood on an isolated farm on the Michigan frontier made her resourceful and hard-working. When she was twelve, her father left the family and her elder brother became ill. Anna took charge, planting crops, chopping wood, and even digging a well. Anna moved to Big Rapids to attend high school. There she started preaching and delivering lectures on temperance, earning the funds to attend Albion College. She continued her studies at Boston University's School of Theology – the only woman in her class. She struggled to get by but got her theology degree in 1878 and became pastor of a congregation in East Dennis, Massachusetts – the first female minister ordained by the Methodist Protestant Church. While working at the church, Anna returned to Boston University and earned a medical degree in 1885, but decided she'd rather work to help women win the right to vote. Encouraged by Susan B. Anthony, Anna started lecturing across the country for women's suffrage.

Anna was a powerful speaker. When the National Woman Suffrage Association (NWSA) and the American Woman Suffrage Association (AWSA) merged into the National American Woman Suffrage Association (NAWSA) in 1890, she became a national lecturer for the organization. She worked for NAWSA for 25 years – speaking at conventions and testifying before committees in Congress, captivating audiences in every state. She was considered the most eloquent speaker in the movement. Anna served as president of NAWSA from 1904 to 1915. Her executive abilities were not as strong and NAWSA was in turmoil when Carrie Chapman returned to head it in 1915. During World War I, Anna chaired the Women's Committee of the Council of National Defense. She received the Distinguished Service Medal in 1919 for her wartime service. After the war, she joined a speaking tour in support of world peace and the new League of Nations. During this tour, she came down with pneumonia and died on July 2, 1919 at the age of 72, one month after Congress passed the 19th Amendment, but 13 months short of its ratification. However, she died knowing that the goal she had spent most of her life working toward had almost been reached.

Fascinating Factoid: Speaking tours were a major tactic of the Women's Suffrage Movement. In September 1915, Sara Bard Field and two Swedish women drove from San Francisco to Washington, D.C. They drove through all kinds of weather in a car covered with women's rights stickers and slogans, changing tires and fixing the car themselves. Everywhere they went, Sara gave speeches and they collected signatures in support of women's suffrage – half a million in all. Four months later when they arrived at the White House and unrolled the petition in front of President Wilson, it was said that the petition stretched for miles. *"We all agreed that it was an impressive meeting and an impressive gesture, but we didn't feel he'd loosened up enough."*

In **Around America to Win the Vote: Two Suffragists, a Kitten, and 10,000 Miles,** Mara Rockliff tells the story of Nell Richardson and Alice Burke – two suffragists on a trek across America. In April 1916, they, their little yellow car and a kitten embarked on a bumpy, muddy, unmapped journey ten thousand miles long , braving blizzards, deserts, and naysayers – not to mention a whole lot of tires stuck in the mud – to spread the word: *"Votes for Women!"*

Read more – *for Kids*: **A Voice From the Wilderness: The Story of Anna Howard Shaw** by Don Brown, 2001. *for Teens and Adults:* **Anna Howard Shaw: The Work of Woman Suffrage** by Trisha Franzen, 2014. **The Story of a Pioneer** by Anna Howard Shaw, 1895.

Visit: Belmont-Paul Women's Equality National Monument Washington DC www.nationalwomansparty.org

Anna Howard Shaw (1847-1919) by Arlene Holmes © 2016
Powerful Speaker for the Women's Suffrage Movement

"A gentleman opposed to their enfranchisement once said to me,
women have never produced anything of any value to the world.
I told him the chief product of the women had been the men,
and left it to him to decide whether the product was of any value."

Harriot Stanton Blatch (1856-1940) – Working Class Suffrage Organizer

Most suffrage activism came from middle and upper class women but Harriot brought working class women into the suffrage movement.

Harriot, the sixth child of Elizabeth Cady Stanton, was born eight years after her mother's speech at the Seneca Falls Convention. Activism was in her blood – both her mother and father were active abolitionists and women's rights advocates. After Harriot graduated from Vassar in 1878 with a degree in mathematics, she attended the Boston School for Oratory for a year, then tutored in Germany. In 1881, Harriot worked with her mother and Susan B. Anthony on the second volume of **The History of Woman Suffrage** and she penned a chapter describing the history of the American Woman Suffrage Association which had split with the National Woman Suffrage Association over the question of the 15th Amendment. Her writing, along with Susan B. Anthony's strong belief that a united movement had a better chance of achieving women's suffrage, would help to bring the two organizations back together.

The following year, she met and married an Englishman and moved to Britain. While there she did a statistical analysis of English villages for which she received a master's degree in mathematics from Vassar College in 1894. She also got involved in women's social reform groups and the activist Women's Suffrage Society, becoming a close friend of its leader, Emmeline Pankhurst.

In 1902, she returned to the states and found that the American women's suffrage movement was floundering. She decided to rejuvenate it by recruiting women workers who had been mostly ignored by the middle-class suffrage movement. In 1907, she established the Equality League of Self-Supporting Women (ELSSW) – an organization that eventually grew to 20,000 women – mostly factory, laundry, and garment workers from the Lower East Side of New York City. Following the British model, they embraced bold new tactics – holding meetings outside and starting suffrage parades – methods that Alice Paul's National Woman's Party would later emulate. Harriot worked hard to bring her friend Emmeline Pankhurst and other British suffragists to speak in the United States. In 1910, her organization became known as the Women's Political Union (WPU). Harriot was a talented political organizer. She managed to mobilize working-class women into parades and militant street protests while simultaneously collaborating with prominent society women and making backroom deals to neutralize the opposition of Tammany Hall politicians who feared (rightly as it turned out) that women would vote for prohibition. In 1913, largely due to her organization's efforts, the New York Legislature passed a suffrage amendment. Four years later it was ratified - making New York the first eastern state to grant women the vote. In 1915, the WPU merged with Alice Paul and Lucy Burns' Congressional Union, which eventually became the National Woman's Party.

Harriot actively supported America's war effort, directing the Food Administration's Speakers Bureau and the Woman's Land Army and publishing **Mobilizing Woman-Power**(1918). After the ratification of the 19th amendment, she worked for the Equal Rights Amendment, the League of Nations, and encouraged women to become involved in peace efforts to stave off any new military conflicts in her book **A Woman's Point of View** (1920). Influenced by socialism in England, Harriot joined the Socialist Party and made an unsuccessful run for comptroller of the City of New York in 1921 and for a Senate seat in 1926. She published her memoir **Challenging Years** in 1940 shortly before her death.

Fascinating Factoid: Harriot's daughter, Nora Stanton Blatch, would follow in her mother's and grandmother's footsteps to become the third generation of Stanton women advocating for women's rights and women's suffrage. Nora studied civil engineering at Cornell University, graduating in 1905. She was the first female member of the American Society of Civil Engineers (ASCE) but was only allowed "junior membership" status because of her gender.

Read More *for adults*: **Harriot Stanton Blatch and the Winning of Woman Suffrage** by Ellen Carol DuBois, 1999.

Visit: National Women's History (Virtual) Museum: www.nwhm.org

Harriot Stanton Blatch (1856-1940) by Amber McGonegal © 2016
Working Class Suffrage Organizer

"Perhaps someday men will raise a tablet reading in letters of gold: 'All honor to women, the first disenfranchised class in history who, unaided by any political party, won enfranchisement by its own effort ... and achieved the victory without the shedding of a drop of human blood. All honor to women of the world!"

Inez Milholland (1886 –1916)
"White Knight" and Martyr for the Women's Suffrage Movement

Inez was born into a wealthy and progressive-minded family. Both her parents were active in world peace, civil rights, and women's rights movements and believed girls could and should get a good education. Inez attended schools in New York City, London, and Berlin before returning to the states to attend college at Vassar. There she organized a suffrage club and soon gained the reputation as liberal activist and firebrand. When the college forbade suffrage meetings, Inez and others scheduled "classes" on the subject along with protests and petition drives. After graduation in 1909, she applied to study law at Yale, Harvard, and Cambridge – but all refused to admit a woman. Finally, she was accepted by New York University and she got her law degree in 1912. After passing her bar exam, she joined a New York law firm. One of her first cases involved conditions at Sing Sing prison. At the time the notion of a woman going into the prison was shocking, yet not only did she insist on talking directly with prisoners, but she also had herself handcuffed to one to see what it felt like to be an inmate.

All though college, law school, and her work as a lawyer, Inez was an activist for labor rights, African American equality, and Socialist causes. Though white, she was a member of the National Association for the Advancement of Colored People. However she gave her most time and energy to the women's suffrage movement. Along with Alice Paul and Lucy Burns, Inez became a leader and a popular speaker for the National Woman's Party, a radical offshoot of the National American Woman Suffrage Association (NAWSA). She argued that women should have the right to vote because they would become the *"house-cleaners of the nation"* and thus would eliminate sweatshops, tenements, prostitution, hunger, poverty, and child mortality.

Inez attended her first suffrage parade on May 7, 1911 holding a sign that read, *"Forward, out of error, Leave behind the night, Forward through the darkness, Forward into light!"* Photogenic and articulate, she soon became the young and beautiful face of the suffrage campaign – the **New York Sun** wrote *"No suffrage parade was complete without Inez Milholland."*

On March 3,1913, the day before President Wilson's inauguration, 27-year-old Inez Milholland cemented her image as the iconic figure of the movement. Riding astride a large white horse, wearing a crown and a long white cape like a modern-day Joan of Arc, she led a suffrage parade down Pennsylvania Avenue through Washington D.C. Behind her were nine bands, five mounted brigades, 26 floats, and 5,000-8,000 marchers including women from Canada, India, Australia, New Zealand and many other countries. However, black women were segregated to mollify white women delegations from the South. The dignitaries included Helen Keller who marched then spoke at Constitution Hall and Jeannette Rankin, who marched proudly under Montana's state sign then returned to Washington, D.C. four years later as the first U.S. congresswoman.

Though many of the estimated 500,000 people along the route were supportive, the marchers also encountered jeering and angry crowds. Many police officers were of little help – some even participated in the harassment. Eventually, young men from the Maryland Agricultural College created a human barrier to protect the women. Over 200 people were treated for injuries at local hospitals. Congress later held an investigation, and the chief of police was fired.

Inez continued to be an active speaker for the National Woman's Party for the rest of her short life, travelling around the country even though she was quite ill with pernicious anemia. On October 22, 1916, she collapsed in the middle of a speech in Los Angeles. She died a month later. Her last public words were, *"Mr. President, how long must women wait for liberty?"* Her sister Vida continued her suffrage work and was imprisoned for three days in 1917.

Read More –*for Teens and Adults:* Remembering Inez: The Last Campaign of Inez Milholland, Suffrage Martyr edited by Robert P. J., Jr. Cooney, 2015. **Inez: The Life and Times of Inez Milholland** by Linda J. Lumsden, 2004. **DVD: Iron Jawed Angels** (HBO, 2004.)

Visit: Belmont-Paul Women's Equality National Monument Washington DC www.nationalwomansparty.org

Inez Milholland (1886 –1916) by Tish Wells © 2016 TishWells14.com
"White Knight" and Martyr for the Women's Suffrage Movement

"I am prepared to sacrifice every so-called privilege I possess in order to have a few rights."

Fascinating Factoid: In 1915, shortly after the *RMS Lusitania* had been torpedoed by a German U-boat, Inez sailed to Italy. Upon landing, the captain informed her that a German submarine had followed them across the ocean. Undeterred, she became a war correspondent and lobbied to be allowed to visit the front lines in the war. However the Italian government was not pleased with her anti-war articles and she was evicted from the country.

Official program for the Woman Suffrage Procession in Washington D.C. March 3, 1913

Washington
D.C.
March 3, 1913

Alice Paul (1885-1977)
Feminist, Suffragist, and Political Strategist

On March 3, 1913, the day before Woodrow Wilson was sworn in as president, half a million people watched at least 5000 women march down Pennsylvania Avenue carrying flags and banners with the message *"Give Women the Vote!"* At the lead was Inez Milholland, sitting astride a white horse, in white flowing Joan of Arc robes, but the woman who had organized the parade was 28-year-old Quaker suffragist Alice Paul. Alice felt the time was right to bring publicity to their cause – over the last few years, many states in the western United States had granted women the right to vote, why shouldn't women in the other states have it too?

Alice had been drawn into the British suffrage movement while attending graduate school in England. She had met the leaders of the movement and became an activist suffragette. She was arrested for helping to organize women into trade unions and sent to jail for "disturbing the peace." After she returned to the states in 1910, she was invited to join the National American Woman Suffrage Association (NAWSA). Deciding that NAWSA's approach of patient speechmaking was not radical enough, Alice and other American suffragettes formed the Congressional Union for Woman Suffrage and later the National Woman's Party (NWP). More protest marches followed. The women were jailed but they did not back down. Alice said *"Once you put your hand to the plough you don't remove it until you get to the end of the row."* Starting In January 1917, they increased the pressure on the President to support the amendment. Over 1000 women from all over the country picketed in front of the White House day and night for months. At least 265 were arrested and jailed. Alice was given solitary confinement in the mental ward. She and many others were cruelly force-fed. They were not allowed visitors or messages.

Ironically, it was this harsh treatment that led to their success. When the newspapers published smuggled accounts of their terrible treatment, public outrage persuaded President Wilson to pardon the suffragists. On January 10, 1918, he gave a speech to the House of Representatives urging them to support the amendment. Seventeen months later, on June 4, 1919, the 19th Amendment granting women the right to vote in national elections passed in Congress. The following year – after fourteen more months of speeches, pickets, and arrests – it was ratified. Alice became a lawyer in 1922 and continued to work for women's rights the rest of her life.

Fascinating Factoids: The 19th amendment needed to be ratified (approved) by two thirds of the states. By late August 1920, it had been ratified by 35 of the 36 states needed. Then on August 26th Tennessee voted – 48 "yea" and 48 "nay" – a tie that meant defeat. But Senator Harry Burn remembered a note his mother **Mrs. J. L. Burn** had sent : *"Don't forget to be a good boy and help Mrs. Catt* put 'Rat' in Ratification."* He changed his vote to "yea" and, 72 years after the Seneca Falls Convention, women finally had the right to vote!

The 19th Amendment legally gave all women, white and black, the right to vote. However, in less than ten years state laws and vigilante practices effectively removed that right from most black women in the South. It would take another 40 years and the activists from the Civil Rights Movement of the 1960s before black women in the South actually could exercise their right to vote.

Read More – *for Kids:* **Miss Paul and the President: The Creative Campaign for Women's Right to Vote** by Dean Robbins, 2016. **Alice Paul** by Elizabeth Raum, 2004. **With Courage and Cloth: Winning the Fight for Women's Right to Vote by** Ann Bauman, 2004. *for Teens and Adults:* **A Woman's Crusade: Alice Paul and the Battle for the Ballot** by Mary Walton, 2010. **DVD: Iron-Jawed Angels** (HBO, 2004) **One Woman, One Vote** (PBS, 2006)

Visit: Belmont-Paul Women's Equality National Monument Washington DC www.nationalwomansparty.org
Paulsdale Mt. Laurel, NJ www.alicepaul.org
New Jersey Women's Heritage Trail www.state.nj.us/dep/hpo/1identify/whttrail2.htm
National Women's History Museums nwhm.org/online-exhibits/rightsforwomen/AfricanAmericanwomen.html

*Carrie Chapman Catt, leader of the National Woman Suffrage Movement

Alice Paul (1885-1977) Feminist, Suffragist, and Political Strategist by Laura Davidson © 2016

"Most reforms, most problems are complicated.
But to me, there is nothing complicated about ordinary equality."

After her fight for women's suffrage, Alice turned her attention to passage of an Equal Rights Amendment that she wrote and sent to Congress in 1923. Nearly 100 years later, it has still not become law in the United States. However due to her efforts, in 1945 the United Nations included equal rights in its charter. It is considered an "international bill of rights for women." In 1979, the United Nations adopted the Convention on the Elimination of Discrimination against Women (CEDAW) to end discrimination, establish equality and work to eliminate violence against women. Nearly all the 193 member states of the United Nations have ratified it. Only seven have not: Iran, Palau, Somalia, South Sudan, Sudan, Tonga and the United States!

Advocates for worker, immigrant, women's and civil rights:

- Emma Lazarus (1849-1887) – Poet and Activist for Immigrant Rights

- Ida Bell Wells-Barnett (1862-1931) – African-American Journalist and Anti-Lynching Activist

- Mary Church Terrell (1863-1954) –   Suffrage Activist and First President of the National Association of Colored Women

- Nellie Bly (1864-1922) – Investigative Journalist who Wrote Exposé on Women Falsely Institutionalized for Madness

- Juliette Gordon Low (1860-1927) – Founded the Girl Scouts of America with the Goal of Helping Girls Become Independent and Self-Reliant

- Margaret Sanger (1883-1966) – Thrown in Jail in 1916 after Opening the First U.S. Birth-Control Clinic

- Rose Schneiderman (1884-1972) –   Labor Organizer and Founder of the Ladies Garment Workers Association

- Elizabeth Gurley Flynn (1890-1964) – "Rebel Girl" and "East Side Joan of Arc"

- Francis Perkins (1880-1965) – Secretary of Labor and First Woman Cabinet Minister in the U.S. Government

- Zitkala-Ša (1876–1938) – Native American and Women's Rights Activist

- Elouise Pepion Cobell (1945-2011) – Tribal Activist who Worked to Restore Funds Owed to Native Americans

- Rosa Parks (1913-2005) – "The First Lady of Civil Rights"

- Septima Poinsette Clark (1898-1987) – "Freedom's Teacher" Founder of Citizenship Schools to Enable Black Voters to Overcome Voting Barriers

- Ella Baker (1903-1986) – "Unsung Heroine of the Civil Rights Movement"

- Fannie Lou Hamer (1917-1977) – African American Voting and Civil Rights Activist

- Dolores Huerta (1930-) – Labor Leader, Women's and Migrant Rights Advocate

- Betty Friedan (1921-2006) – Groundbreaking Author of the 1963 Book *The Feminine Mystique* Which Kicked off a New Wave of Feminism

- Gloria Steinem (1934-) – Founder of Ms. Magazine and Outspoken Champion for the "Second Wave" of the Women's Rights Movement

- Marian Wright Edelman (1939-) –   Founder of the Children's Defense Fund

Emma Lazarus (1849-1887) Poet and Activist for Immigrant Rights

"Until we are all free, we are none of us free."

Emma grew up in New York City, a privileged daughter of a wealthy sugar refiner. Her father, contrary to the general opinion of the day, believed girls could and should learn, and he hired tutors for Emma, her brother and five sisters. Emma loved reading, especially poetry, and began to write her own poems. Inspired by a visit to a 100-year-old synagogue built by Spanish and Portuguese Jews who, like her own family, had sought refuge in America after fleeing their homelands, Emma wrote:

> *What prayers were in this temple offered up,*
> *Wrung from sad hearts that knew no joy on earth,*
> *By these lone exiles of a thousand years,*
> *From the fair sunrise land that gave them birth!*

Her father had her poems printed in "***Poems and translations by Emma Lazarus, written between the ages of Fourteen and Seventeen***" and the following year a publishing company published her book. Over the next few years, she published two more books of poetry as well as poems, essays, and book reviews in magazines. One of her editors introduced her to a politician, William Evarts. He invited her to attend a mass protest rally. It was an event that would change her life.

In a hall crowded with people, Mr. Evarts told of the horrifying plight of the Jews of Russia – of pograms – mobs roving from town to town burning down Jewish homes, stealing their belongings, beating and sometimes even killing Jews. He spoke of shiploads of Russian Jews escaping this violence who were arriving daily and who were being housed in temporary barracks on Ward's Island in New York Harbor. When Emma visited the barracks, she was shocked to see thousands of refugees, hungry, scared, crowded together, kids playing among garbage, families being fed soup crawling with worms. Outraged, Emma wrote an article in the newspaper telling of what she'd seen. She collected money, brought food and clothing, helped start English and occupational classes, and met with government officials to try to improve conditions. She was especially upset that many Americans wanted new laws to keep the immigrants out – blaming them for crime, disease, and poverty. Outraged at this injustice, she wrote articles, plays, and poems advocating for the immigrants.

She traveled to England and on her trip home as she sailed into New York Harbor, she thought about how different the welcome she would receive from family and friends was compared to the ones immigrants received on their arrival. On her return, she had a letter from Mr. Evarts. He told her that France had sent the U.S. a huge statue called "Liberty Enlightening the World" but it was in a warehouse because it lacked a base. He was holding an auction to raise funds and he wondered if she would write a poem for the event. At first Emma refused – she didn't write poems to order, they came from her heart – and the auction was next week, she couldn't write one in that short of a time. But as she thought about the Russian immigrants and her own great-great-grandfather, she had an idea. She imagined the immigrants seeing the enormous statue in the harbor – a woman with a light welcoming the newcomers. And she wrote her famous lines: "*Give me your tired, your poor, Your huddled masses yearning to breathe free...*"

Sadly, Emma died in 1887. She didn't live to see her poem installed on the base of the Statue of Liberty in 1903 – or know that her words would be on the lips of generations of people around the world.

Read More – *for Kids:* **Liberty's Voice** by Erica Silverman, 2011. **Emma's Poem: The Voice of the Statue of Liberty** by Linda Glaser, 2010 (Jane Addams Award Book). *for Teens and Adults:* **Emma Lazarus** by Esther Schor, 2006. **Lady Liberty: The Untold Story of the Statue of Liberty** by Lenore Skomal, 2009.

Visit: The Statue of Liberty National Monument New York Harbor www.nps.gov/stli/learn/historyculture/emma-lazarus.htm

Emma Lazarus by Sheryl Depp © 2016   primarilyartwithmrsdepp.blogspot.com

Mother of Exiles....Give me your tired, your poor,
Your huddled masses yearning to breathe free,
The wretched refuse of your teeming shore.
Send these, the homeless, tempest-tost to me,
I lift my lamp beside the golden door!"

Ida Bell Wells-Barnett (1862-1931)
African-American Journalist and Anti-Lynching Activist

Ida Bell was born in the middle of the Civil War. After the war was over and her family was free, her father opened his own carpentry shop and helped to found Shaw College – a new school for free African-Americans. Ida studied there but at age 16, she was forced to quit school when both her parents died in a yellow fever epidemic. To support her five younger siblings, Ida became a teacher traveling six miles each week to teach, then coming home each weekend to cook, clean, and look after the house.

From the start, Ida wasn't afraid to stand up (or sit down) for what was right. On May 4, 1884 (70 years before Rosa Parks' similar action on a bus), a train conductor ordered Ida to give up her seat in the first-class ladies car and move to the crowded second-class smoking car reserved for African Americans. Ida refused and the conductor and two men dragged her out. When she returned to Memphis, she wrote a newspaper article in a black church paper about her treatment on the train and hired two different lawyers to sue the railroad – and she won! On December 24, 1884 the local circuit court granted her a $500 award, but in 1877 the Tennessee Supreme Court reversed the lower court's ruling, concluding, *"We think it is evident that the purpose of the defendant in error was to harass with a view to this suit, and that her persistence was not in good faith to obtain a comfortable seat for the short ride."* Ida was ordered to pay court costs. She wrote: *"I felt so disappointed because I had hoped such great things from my suit for my people...O God, is there no...justice in this land for us?"*

Unwilling to be silenced, Ida became co-owner of Memphis **Free Speech** newspaper and wrote articles about other injustices against African Americans that were published in papers across the country. After three of her friends were lynched (killed by a mob), Ida began researching the reasons why. She found that, contrary to the claim that black men were being killed because they had committed violent crimes, the real reason for their murders was because white men feared that African Americans would take their jobs or cut into their profits. She published *"A Red Record"* and *"Southern Horrors: Lynch Law in All Its Phases"* documenting thousands of lynchings of African Americans and the racist laws that supported this violence and she urged black families to leave Memphis and move to Oklahoma territory. Thousands followed her advice but Ida stayed – carrying a pistol for self-defense. Finally after a mob attacked her newspaper office and threatened to lynch her, Ida moved to New York City and then Chicago, where she married a lawyer, raised four children and continued writing articles and speaking out against lynching and for rights for African Americans and women's suffrage. She became the first president of the Negro Fellowship League in 1900, helped found the National Association for the Advancement of Colored People in 1909 and remained active and militant her whole life.

Fascinating Factoid: For 18 years after the Civil War ended, most Southern states had civil rights laws. However in 1883, the U.S. Supreme Court ruled that the federal Civil Rights Act of 1875 was unconstitutional. Southern states lost no time in writing new "Jim Crow" laws denying Black Americans admittance to or forcing them to use separate sections of restaurants, hotels, libraries, theaters, buses, water fountains, and other public and private facilities. Sadly, a similar situation occurred more recently when in 2013 the Supreme Court struck down a section of the 1965 Voting Rights Act – states adopted voter ID and other regulations that make it harder for minorities and poor people to vote.

Read more – *for Kids:* **Ida B. Wells: Let the Truth Be Told** by Walter Dean Myers, 2008. **Yours for Justice, Ida B. Wells: The Daring Life of a Crusading Journalist** by Philip Dray, 2008. **Ida B. Wells: Mother of the Civil Rights Movement** by Dennis Brindell Fradin, 2000. *for Teens and Adults:* **Crusade for Justice: The Autobiography of Ida B. Wells**, 1930. **Ida: A Sword Among Lions: Ida B. Wells and the Campaign Against Lynching** by Paula J. Giddings, 2008.

Visit: Wells-Barnett Museum Holly Springs, MI www.ibwfoundation.org/Wells-Barnett_Museum.html

Ida Bell Wells-Barnett (1862-1931) by Mary Delaney Connelly © 2016
African-American Journalist and Anti-Lynching Activist

"The way to right wrongs is to turn the light of truth upon them."

"The awful death-roll that Judge Lynch is calling every week is appalling, not only because of the lives it takes, the cruelty and outrage to the victims, but because of the prejudice it fosters." (Southern Horrors, 1892.)

Mary Church Terrell (1863-1954) Suffrage Activist
First President of the National Association of Colored Women

Mary grew up in Memphis, Tennessee. Her parents were former slaves and her father had become wealthy investing in real estate – some sources say he was the first black millionaire in the South. Both of her parents believed strongly in the value of education. When she was six, they sent her off to Antioch Model School in Ohio. After she graduated, she continued on to Oberlin College, the first in the nation to admit women and African Americans. Mary was one of the first black women to enroll. No slouch, she studied Greek, Latin, French, and German, was elected to two college literary societies and as an editor of *The Oberlin Review*. She got her Bachelor's degree in 1884, then a earned a master's degree in mathematics in 1888. Her father disapproved of women working, but Mary became a university professor in Ohio and a school principal in Washington DC, until she had to resign when she married in 1891.

The direction of Mary's life changed the following year when a friend of hers was lynched in Memphis. Mary and noted African American activist Frederick Douglass spoke with President Benjamin Harrison about the increasing racial violence but he did nothing. Frederick Douglass urged her to devote her talents toward organizing for racial justice. Mary began organizing African-American women's clubs, and in 1896, she was elected as the first president of the National Association of Colored Women. In that role, she toured the country, lecturing on African-American history, advocating for educational opportunities, and setting up local women's suffrage chapters. Using the pen name "Euphemia Kirk," she also wrote articles in a variety of newspapers to promote the movement . She became the first African-American woman ever appointed to a school board and then served on a committee that investigated alleged police mistreatment of African Americans. In 1904 Mary was invited to speak at the International Congress of Women held in Berlin, Germany. She was the only black woman at the conference. She received an enthusiastic ovation when she honored the host nation by delivering her address in German. She then delivered the speech in French, and concluded with the English version. In 1909, Mary and journalist Ida B. Wells-Barnett were the only black women invited to attend the first organizational meeting of the National Association for the Advancement of Colored People (NAACP). Mary remained an activist for African-American women all her long life. In 1949, she sued the American Association of University Women after they denied her admission. After being refused service by a whites-only restaurant in 1950, Mary and several other activists picketed and sued the establishment. In 1954,the U.S. Supreme Court ruled that discrimination based on race in public places in Washington D.C. was illegal, laying the groundwork for Rosa Parks' case two years later.

Nannie Helen Burroughs (1878 –1961) was another African-American educator, orator, feminist, and civil rights activist. A strong advocate of poor and working-class black women, she urged the unionization of domestic workers because "the women voters will be keen to see that laws are passed that will give eight hours a day…to women in other industries, but they will oppose any movement that will, in the end, prevent them from keeping their cooks and house servants in the kitchen twelve or fifteen hours a day."

Fascinating Factoid: Segregated women's clubs were the norm in America. The motto of the General Federation of Women's Clubs was "unity in diversity" but women of color were not admitted, so they formed their own clubs. The National Association of Colored Women (NACW) incorporated in 1896 had 50,000 members by 1917. Mexican-American women, inspired by Latina journalist Jovita Idar de Juarez, formed La Liga Feminil Mexicanista. The suffrage movement was similarly racially divided. The National American Woman Suffrage Association (NAWSA) and even the more radical National Woman's Party (NWP), worried about angering white Southern suffragist women, often excluded black women from the movement, so African-American women formed their own suffrage organizations in many parts of the country (though some black leaders worked with the NAWSA).

Read More – *for Kids and Teens:* **Mary Church Terrell: Leader for Equality** by Patricia and Fredrick McKissack, 2002. **Fight On!: Mary Church Terrell's Battle for Integration** by Dennis and Judith Fradin, 2003. *for Adults:* **Just Another Southern Town: Mary Church Terrell and the Struggle for Racial Justice in the Nation's Capital** by Joan Quigley, 2016. **A Colored Woman In A White World** by Mary Church Terrell, 1940.

Visit: Mary Church Terrill House (part of Washington DC Civil Rights Trail)
www.nps.gov/nr/travel/civilrights/dc2.htm

Mary Church Terrell (1863-1954) by Mary Delaney Connelly © 2016

*"I cannot help wondering sometimes what I might have become and might have done
if I had lived in a country which had not circumscribed and handicapped me on account of my race,
that had allowed me to reach any height I was able to attain."*

Elizabeth Cochrane Seaman – aka Nellie Bly (1864-1922) Investigative Journalist

Some women fought for changes for women with lectures and petitions, Nellie Bly used another technique – investigative journalism. She is credited as largely inventing the field of investigative reporting. Resourceful and courageous, she would pose as a lunatic, prostitute, chorus girl, sweatshop worker and shoplifter to get inside stories on the horrible conditions facing women.

Elizabeth's father was a prominent businessman and judge in Pennsylvania. However, he died when she was six and she and her siblings grew up in poverty since he had made no provision for them in his will. After lack of money for schooling thwarted her plans to become a teacher, she helped her mother run a boarding house. In 1885, at age 20, she wrote an angry letter to the editor of **The Pittsburgh Dispatch** rebutting a columnist's assertion that women were unfit for anything except domestic tasks. Impressed by her writing, the newspaper hired her and gave her the pen name "Nellie Bly." Nellie wrote hard-hitting stories about the hardships facing poor working-class girls and about reform of the state's divorce law – something she knew about firsthand from her mother's divorce from her abusive second husband. However, frustrated that most of her assignments were about flower shows and fashion, Nellie moved to New York.

After six months looking for a job at a newspaper, Nellie finally convinced **The New York World** to hire her. Nellie's first assignment was to write about the mentally ill in New York City. Instead of doing interviews, Nellie decided to go undercover – pretending to be insane, she was admitted into the Women's Lunatic Asylum on Blackwell's Island. She lived at the institution for 10 days, observing physical cruelty, ice-cold baths, and forced meals of rancid food. After her lawyer obtained her release, her report led to public outcry, a grand jury investigation of the institution and reforms in patient care (though men could still have their "uppity" wives institutionalized for madness without real proof well into the twentieth century). Nellie did similar investigative pieces on women's prisons, sweatshops, and conditions facing prostitutes and chorus girls. Though some other journalists called it "stunt reporting," Nellie's investigative reporting style was effective and popular with the public and papers alike. People called her "the best reporter in America."

Looking for another challenge, in 1889 Nellie decided to best the record of Phileas Fogg, the fictional adventurer in Jules Verne's best-selling novel **Around the World in 80 Days**. Sailing from Hoboken, NJ on November 14, 1889, her day-by-day account as she circled the globe by boat, train, burro and rickshaw was featured on the front page of the **New York World** – riveting readers. When she arrived back in New York City, 72 days, 6 hours and 11 minutes later, she was celebrated with screaming crowds, a grand parade and fireworks display. A year later, Nellie married wealthy businessman Robert Seaman – a week after meeting him! When he died ten years later, she ran his business – turning his industries into multimillion-dollar companies and putting her social reforms into practice by paying her workers well and providing them with gymnasiums, libraries, and health care. During World War I, she returned to reporting and was the only woman on the Eastern Front. She was a reporter until her death in 1922 at the age of 58.

Fascinating Factoid: Unbeknownst to her, a few hours after Nellie departed on her around the world challenge, Elisabeth Bisland, a **Cosmopolitan** columnist, set off in the opposite direction. Their competitive journeys are told in Matthew Goodman's book: **Eighty Days: Nellie Bly and Elizabeth Bisland's History-Making Race Around the World** (2013).

Read More – *for Kids:* **Bylines: A Photobiography of Nellie Bly** by Sue Macy and Linda Ellerbee, 2009. **Nellie Bly and Investigative Journalism for Kids: Mighty Muckrakers from the Golden Age to Today** by Ellen Mahoney, 2015. *for Teens and Adults:* **Ten Days a Madwoman: The Daring Life and Turbulent Times of the Original "Girl" Reporter, Nellie Bly** by Deborah Noyes, 2016. **Around the World in Seventy-Two Days and Other Writings** by Nellie Bly.

Nellie Bly (1864-1922) Investigative Journalist by Natalie Obedos © 2016 yellowfences@tumblr.com

"How can a doctor judge a woman's sanity by merely bidding her good morning and refusing to hear her pleas for release? Even the sick ones know it is useless to say anything, for the answer will be that it is their imagination."

"I hardly expected the grand jury to sustain me, after they saw everything different from what it had been while I was there. Yet they did, and their report to the court advises all the changes made that I had proposed."

Juliette Gordon Low (1860-1927)   Founded the Girl Scouts of America
Promoted Self-Reliance in Girls

"Together we can create a better world."

When Juliette was a little girl, she heard stories about her great-grandmother Eleanor Lytle McKillip who had been kidnapped and adopted by the Seneca. Chief Cornplanter had given his strong and independent new daughter a new name "Little-Ship-Under-Full-Sail." It was a nickname Juliette's family would give her as well since she went through life *"proudly and fearlessly, in spite of strong winds and stormy seas."* Juliette would later tell her great-grandmother's story often – especially to Girl Scouts around a campfire.

Juliette spent her childhood in Savannah, Georgia. Her father was a Southerner, her mother a Yankee from Chicago who had met her future husband when she slid down the banister while visiting the library at Yale University – flattening his hat! The Civil War broke out just a few months after "Daisy" (as she was affectionately called) was born. In spite of the hardships all around, she and her cousins made their own fun. She was dubbed "Crazy Daisy" by her family and friends because of her many crazy schemes. One cousin remarked *"While you never knew what she would do next, she always did what she made up her mind to do."* When Juliette was 20 years old, she got an earache. A botched treatment led to the loss of much of her hearing in that ear. Undeterred by this disability, she traveled in Europe and eventually married a British aristocrat. At the wedding, a grain of rice landed in Juliette's other ear which caused an infection that eventually left her completely deaf in that ear.

Though they had impressive houses in London and Scotland, it wasn't a happy marriage. Her husband drank and gambled and Juliette found out she couldn't have children. She looked for happiness in other ways. When she wanted a new gate for her house, she learned metalworking and forged it herself. She hosted lively parties and was known for her sense of fun – once she sneaked out of a fancy dinner party to go fishing in her finery with her friend Rudyard Kipling! She also traveled widely – riding elephants in India, seeing the pyramids in Egypt, and even flying in one of the new aeroplanes which she called *"a delicious experience."* But Daisy grew restless. She wanted to do something useful that made a difference in people's lives. In 1911, she met Sir Robert Baden-Powell. He had started the Boy Scouts in England and his sister had created a similar organization called Girl Guides. Daisy loved the idea! Returning to Savannah the next year, she telephoned a cousin and announced, *"I've got something for the girls of Savannah, and all of America, and all the world, and we're going to start it tonight!"*

On March 12, 1912, Daisy stood before 18 girls at America's first Girl Scout meeting to tell them about the adventures they would have. She then designed uniforms with bloomers for them to wear so they could play basketball in the vacant lot across the street and go hiking and boating and camping. At night they sang songs around the campfire and slept under the stars. She co-wrote a manual to encourage them to earn badges as they learned new skills. Daisy traveled across America to publicize her idea and encourage new troops. From the start, her Girl Scout organization was open and inclusive. Juliette broke the conventions of the time—reaching across class, cultural, and ethnic boundaries to ensure all girls, including those with so-called disabilities, had a place to grow and develop their leadership skills. Troops were organized in schools and in synagogues, in factories and in orphanages, in churches and communities across the country. Using her talent for fundraising and public relations, along with a vast network of friends and supporters, Daisy led the Girl Scouts for over a decade with passion and determination—telling the girls she met that they could be doctors or scientists, architects or airline pilots, *"One of you...may someday alter the lives of hundreds of thousands of people."*

Read more (a sampling) *for Kids and Teens:* **Here Come the Girl Scouts!** by Shana Corey, 2012. **First Girl Scout: The Life of Juliette Gordon Low,** by Ginger Wadsworth, 2012. **Daisy and the Girl Scouts: The Story of Juliette Gordon Low** by Fern Brown, 1996. *for Teens and Adults:* **Juliette Gordon Low: The Remarkable Founder of the Girl Scouts** by Stacy A. Cordery, 2012. **Lady from Savannah** by Daisy Gordon Lawrence, 1958.

I will do my best to be honest and fair, friendly and helpful, considerate and caring, courageous and strong, and responsible for what I say and do, and to respect myself and others, respect authority, use resources wisely, make the world a better place, and be a sister to every Girl Scout.

The work of today is the history of tomorrow and we are its makers.

Juliette Gordon Low (1860-1927) by Jody Flegal © 2016

Fascinating Factoid: All her life, Daisy loved nature and animals. She adopted many starving cats and dogs which she faithfully cared for. As a girl, she pinned a guest room coverlet around a shivering cow one freezing night – her mom was furious when she found the coverlet trampled on the stable floor the next morning! As an adult, she handed a $5 tip to a horse-drawn cab-driver – telling him to *"give that bag of bones of yours a good meal."*

Visit: Juliette Gordon Low Birthplace Savannah GA www.juliettegordonlowbirthplace.org
Girl Scout Visitor Center New York City www.girlscouts.org/en/visit-us/visit-us.html

Margaret Sanger (1883-1966)
Founder of the Modern Birth Control Movement

Born into a family of 11 children, Margaret saw first-hand how her mother struggled to feed and provide for her children and how each additional pregnancy took a terrible toll on her mother's health and led to her early death at age 50. In 1910, Margaret became a visiting nurse and midwife in the slums of the Lower East Side. There she saw women enduring pregnancy after pregnancy. They had no information on how to prevent unwanted pregnancies.

In 1910, birth control devices were illegal and the Comstock Law of 1873 had made distributing information by mail illegal too. Margaret tried to find information in public libraries, but there was none to be found. Distressed by the death of one of her patients, Margaret vowed *"I would tell the world what was going on in the lives of these poor women. No matter what it should cost, I would be heard."* She began a campaign to challenge governmental censorship by deliberately distributing contraceptive information. In 1914 Margaret launched ***The Woman Rebel***, an eight-page monthly newsletter which promoted "birth control" (a term she popularized). That August, she was indicted for violating postal obscenity laws by sending the ***The Woman Rebel*** through the postal system. Rather than stand trial, she sailed to England. She spent a year in Europe researching what people there were using for family planning. When she returned, the case was dismissed – she was free, but the law was still on the books. In 1916, she and her sister Ethel Byrne opened a birth control clinic in Brooklyn – the first in the United States. Thousands of women lined up to receive birth control information and devices. Almost immediately the clinic was shut down and Margaret and Ethel were arrested for keeping a "public nuisance." In jail, they were treated terribly – Margaret was sent to a workhouse for 30 days and Ethel went on a hunger strike and was force-fed – but the publicity turned out to be good for the cause. Their arrest, trial, and appeal sparked birth control activism across the United States, earning the support of many donors who would provide funding and support in the future. In 1918, the birth control movement won a victory when the New York Court of Appeals issued a ruling allowing doctors to prescribe contraception.

Margaret spent the rest of her life working to legalize birth control. In 1921, she created the American Birth Control League (which became Planned Parenthood Federation of America in 1942), and in 1952 she became the first president of the International Planned Parenthood Association. That same year she persuaded Katherine McCormick, a wealthy scientist and feminist, to fund research to develop an oral contraceptive ("the pill") which would change women's lives when it came on the market in the 1960s. In total, Margaret spent more than 50 years battling governments, the medical profession and religious leaders for the right for women to control their own bodies.

Fascinating Factoid: Decades after Margaret Sanger started her birth control campaign, contraception still remained illegal in many parts of the country. It only became widely available in 1965 when the U.S. Supreme Court ruled in Griswold v. Connecticut that contraception was a constitutional right for married couples. (Unmarried couples had to wait until 1972.) In 1973, the Supreme Court's landmark decision to legalize abortion in "Roe v. Wade" on the grounds of a "right to privacy" sparked a backlash that continues to this day.

Read More – *for Kids:* **Margaret Sanger "Every Child a Wanted Child"** by Nancy Whitelaw, 1994. *for Teens and Adults:* **Woman Rebel: The Margaret Sanger Story** by Peter Bagge, 2013. **Margaret Sanger: A Life of Passion** by Jean H. Baker, 2011. **The Feminist Revolution: A Story of the Three Most Inspiring and Empowering Women in American History: Susan B. Anthony, Margaret Sanger, and Betty Friedan** by Jules Archer and Naomi Wolf, 2015. DVD: **Choices of the Heart: The Margaret Sanger Story.**

Visit: Margaret Sanger's Statue in the National Portrait Gallery's "Struggle for Justice" Exhibit. Washington, DC npg.si.edu/exhibition/struggle-justice
Place setting at Judy Chicago's *Dinner Party* **Brooklyn Museum.** www.brooklynmuseum.org/eascfa/dinner_party

Margaret Sanger (1883-1966) Founder of the Modern Birth Control Movement by Jill Schmidt © 2016

"No woman can call herself free who does not own and control her body. No woman can call herself free until she can choose consciously whether she will or will not be a mother."

"Every child a wanted child."

Rose Schneiderman (1884-1972)
Labor Organizer, Founder of the Ladies Garment Workers Association

Immigrants coming to America dreamed of streets paved with gold but found instead low-paying jobs working in aptly named "sweatshops" under terrible conditions. Rose was one of those immigrants. When she was eight, her Jewish family left Russian Poland and immigrated to the Lower East Side of New York City. Two years later her father died and Rose had to leave school after sixth grade to help earn money for her family. She worked in a department store 70 hours a week for three cents an hour. Long hours and low pay were the norm – especially for women, since labor unions only admitted men. In 1898, when she was fourteen, Rose became a cap maker. Five years later, she was a co-founder of a local chapter of the Hat, Cap, and Millinery Workers for Women and in 1905, she helped organize a citywide capmakers' strike. That brought her in contact with the Women's Trade Union League (WTUL) and two years later, she became a full-time organizer for the WTUL.

Rose was soon recognized as an articulate advocate for women's rights in the workplace. She motivated and stood with the *Uprising of the 20,000*, a massive 14-week strike of New York City shirtwaist workers in 1909 supported by the International Ladies' Garment Workers' Union. The picketers were met with violence – thugs hired by their employers beat the women while police looked the other way. When the Triangle Shirtwaist Factory caught on fire in 1911 and 146 workers – mostly young Jewish and Italian immigrant women – died because the escape doors had been locked by the management, Rose spoke out forcefully at a memorial service: *"I would be a traitor to these poor burned bodies if I came here to talk good fellowship... The life of men and women is so cheap and property is so sacred... I know from my experience it is up to the working people to save themselves. The only way they can save themselves is by a strong working-class movement."*

Rose became president of the WTUL in 1918. For the next 31 years, she led the League as it fought for laws to protect workers, including an eight hour workday and minimum wage. She also organized women workers abroad through her efforts to establish the International Congress of Working Women. She ran for U.S. Senate in 1920 as the Farm Labor candidate. Though she lost, she attracted national attention for working class issues. Rose was a founding member of the American Civil Liberties Union, and became friends with Eleanor and Franklin Roosevelt. During the Great Depression, then President Roosevelt appointed her to his "Brain Trust" and she was a close advisor to him on labor issues. From 1937 to 1944, she was Secretary of Labor for New York State, and campaigned for the extension of social security to domestic workers and for equal pay for female workers. During World War II, she was involved in efforts to rescue European Jews but could only rescue a small number.

Throughout her life, Rose promoted women's rights. She campaigned for women's suffrage as a member of the National American Woman Suffrage Association. To her, votes for women were a critical element of economic rights. When a state legislator warned in 1912 that women in politics would lose their charm, she retorted: *"We have women working in the foundries, stripped to the waist, if you please, because of the heat. Yet the Senator says nothing about these women losing their charm... they are cheaper and work longer hours than men. Women in the laundries stand for 13 or 14 hours in the terrible steam and heat with their hands in hot starch. Surely these women won't lose any more of their beauty and charm by putting a ballot in a ballot box once a year than they are likely to lose standing in foundries or laundries all year round. There is no harder contest than the contest for bread, let me tell you that."*

Read More – *for Kids and Teens:* **Flesh and Blood so Cheap: The Triangle Shirtwaist Fire and its Legacy** by Albert Marrin, 2011. **Fannie Never Flinched: One Woman's Courage in the Struggle for American Labor Union Rights** by Mary Cronk Farrell, 2006. *for Adults:* **Common Sense and a Little Fire: Women and Working-Class Politics in the United States, 1900-1965** by Annelise Orleck, 1995. DVD: **Triangle Fire** (PBS American Experience, 2011).

Visit: Lower East Side Tenement Museum. New York City NY www.tenement.org.
Triangle Fire Open Archive rememberthetrianglefire.org/open-archive

Rose Schneiderman (1884-1972) Labor Organizer, Founder of the Ladies Garment Workers Association
by Mariya Kovalyov © 2016   www.happyfamilyart.com

Fascinating Factoid: The famous political slogan and strike song *"Bread and Roses"* originated in a speech given by Rose Schneiderman where she said *"The worker must have bread, but she must have roses, too"* (calling for both fair wages and dignified working conditions). The slogan inspired the title of the 1911 poem *Bread and Roses* by James Oppenheim. A 1912 textile strike in Lawrence, Massachusetts was nicknamed the "Bread and Roses strike."

Elizabeth Gurley Flynn (1890-1964)
"Rebel Girl" and "East Side Joan of Arc"

Elizabeth's father was a radical Socialist and her mother an active feminist, so perhaps it wasn't surprising that she grew up to be both. When she was just sixteen years old, she gave her first public speech titled "What Socialism Will Do for Women" to an audience at the Harlem Socialist Club. From there she moved on to street corners. Crowds were captivated by the girl with the dark hair and blue eyes who talked about social injustice – the authorities were not. The police arrested Elizabeth for blocking traffic and soon her high school expelled her.

That just gave Elizabeth more time for her political activities. In 1908, she became an organizer for the Industrial Workers of the World (IWW). The IWW was a radical labor union of mostly-immigrant, unskilled workers – workers who were generally refused membership in the existing American Federation of Labor (AFL) which represented mostly American-born skilled craftsmen. She traveled coast to coast for the IWW, galvanizing workers with her speeches. Many of her audiences were male, but in 1912 she helped lead a huge strike of the mostly-female textile workers in Massachusetts. The authorities reacted violently. Many of the women were badly beaten and one was killed when police shot at the demonstrators. Over the course of many worker actions, Elizabeth was arrested ten times, but was never sentenced to prison. Prosecutors had no charges – the police were simply harassing her because the businessmen managing the factories did not want to have unionized workers. But Elizabeth refused to be intimidated and her words gave courage to the workers.

After the United States entered World War I in 1917, Elizabeth was again arrested – accused of spying under the new federal Espionage Act. After a long legal battle, she was acquitted but this experience inspired her to be one of the founders of the American Civil Liberties Union (ACLU) in order to defend free speech and other constitutional rights for all Americans. Elizabeth's views of labor became more radical during the Great Depression of the 1930s. She became a leader in the American branch of the Communist Party, which resulted in her ouster from the ACLU in 1940. But when the U.S. entered World War II, she actively supported the American effort. She advocated for equal economic opportunity and pay for women, both in her feminist column for **The Daily Worker** and in her booklet, **"Women Have a Date with Destiny."** She encouraged women to take war jobs, and she supported the establishment of day care centers for working mothers.

In 1942, Elizabeth ran for Congress from New York on a platform stressing women's issues. She received 50,000 votes but did not win. In 1948 a dozen former leaders of the Communist Party were charged with advocating the overthrow of the U.S. government. When Elizabeth protested their conviction, she too was arrested, tried, convicted and sentenced to two years in prison or deportation to the Soviet Union. Saying she wanted to defend free speech in America, she chose prison and spent her 65th and 66th birthdays at the federal women's prison in Alderson, West Virginia. There she wrote **The Alderson Story: My Life as a Political Prisoner**. After her release from prison, she resumed her advocacy for leftist and Communist causes. In 1960, after the Supreme Court ruled that she could not be denied a passport, she took her first trip to the Soviet Union. In 1961, at age 71, she became the first woman to head the U. S. Communist Party. She was visiting Moscow when she died on September 5, 1964. The Soviet government gave her a state funeral in Red Square and over 25,000 people attended. Then, as per her wishes, her remains were returned to the United States.

Fascinating Factoids: Elizabeth Gurley Flynn was celebrated in Joe Hill's 1915 song *"The Rebel Girl."* Her statement of defense of the first Amendment at her 1952 trial is listed as #87 in American Rhetoric's **Top 100 Speeches of the 20th Century**. A fictionalized version of her character appears in John Updike's novel **In the Beauty of the Lilies**.

Read More – *for Teens and Adults:* **I Speak My Own Piece** by Elizabeth Gurley Flynn, 1955.
Elizabeth Gurley Flynn: Modern American Revolutionary by Lara Vapnek, 2015. **A People's History of the United States** by Howard Zinn, 1980 (also available as a young people's edition).

Elizabeth Gurley Flynn (1890-1964) by Arlene Holmes © 2016 Labor Organizer
(based on sheet music cover for Joe Hill's song "Rebel Girl")

"Is it not much better to even die fighting for something than to have lived an uneventful life, never gotten anything, and leaving conditions the same or worse than they were and to have future generations go through the same misery and poverty and degradation?
The only people whose names are recorded in history are those who did something. The peaceful and indifferent are forgotten, they never know the fighting joy of living." (1917)

Frances Perkins (1880-1965)
First American Woman Cabinet Member* and the Woman Behind the New Deal

Frances was born into a comfortable family and privileged to go to college at a time when such options were rare for women. But once there she got a rude awakening. One of her courses required that she visit a local factory. She was appalled by what she saw – unclean and unsafe working conditions with workers in desperate poverty. In 1911, she witnessed the fire at the Triangle Shirtwaist Factory. Many exits were blocked and she saw many young women were jumping out windows – 146 died, mostly young female immigrants. A state commission hired Frances to investigate. The commission's report led to 36 new laws limiting work hours, setting safety requirements and aid to employees injured on the job.

In 1919 Al Smith was elected Governor of New York. He appointed Frances to the Industrial Commission at the Department of Labor over the objections of many people who thought the job was inappropriate for a woman. Frances was sent to help settle a labor dispute. Copper workers were frustrated by poor wages and no extra pay for overtime – she listened, was able to gain their trust, and brokered a deal without violence. When Franklin Delano Roosevelt was elected Governor in 1928, he supported her work to limit child labor and reduce hours for women workers. In 1932, after he won the presidency, he asked her to become the U.S. Secretary of Labor – a critical position since the country was in the midst of the Great Depression. Though torn by family obligations (her husband was ill and her teenage daughter was reluctant to move to Washington D.C.), Frances ultimately said yes. She was the country's first female cabinet member.

When Frances arrived in Washington, millions of Americans were out of work and out of hope. She pushed for massive public works projects to create millions of jobs for unemployed workers. She visited steel works and dockyards. She supported labor unions and a living wage and, as head of the Immigration Service, she fought to bring European refugees to safety in the United States. Her most important work was spearheading the Social Security Act of 1935 and the Fair Labor Act of 1938 – these guaranteed income to unemployed or retired workers, a minimum wage and maximum hours and ended child labor. All these reforms became known as the "New Deal." Frances remained Labor Secretary for 13 years and later became an author, speaker, and professor at Cornell University. She remained an advocate for labor and women's rights all her life.

Fascinating Factoid: In the Great Depression, many businesses and even government agencies wouldn't hire married women. The Economy Act of 1932 explicitly stated that if a husband and wife both worked for the Federal Government and the government had to make layoffs, the wife should be let go. In addition to being unfair, this bias hurt families who often needed both salaries to live on.

Read More (a sampling) *for Kids:* **Ladies First: 40 Daring American Women Who Were Second to None** by Elizabeth Cody Kimmel, 2006. *for Teens and Adults:* **The Woman Behind the New Deal: The Life and Legacy of Frances Perkins** by Kirstin Downey, 2009. **The Roosevelt I Knew** by Frances Perkins, 1946. **Flesh and Blood So Cheap: The Triangle Fire and Its Legacy** by Albert Marrin, 2011.

Visit: Frances Perkins Center Newcastle, ME   francesperkinscenter.org

*To date, the United States has had 30 female cabinet secretaries. In 1953, 20 years after Frances became a cabinet secretary, President Dwight Eisenhower appointed **Oveta Culp Hobby** as the second female cabinet member to head the new Department of Health, Education, and Welfare. It was another 24 years before Jimmy Carter appointed a third woman to the cabinet. **Patricia Roberts Harris**, the first African-American female, was his Secretary of Housing and Urban Development. **Elizabeth Dole** was appointed by Ronald Reagan as Secretary of Transportation in 1983, and later Secretary of Labor for George H. W. Bush. **Madeleine Albright** became the first foreign-born woman Cabinet member when Bill Clinton appointed her Secretary of State in 1997, he also appointed **Janet Reno** as the first female Attorney General. When **Condoleezza Rice** became Secretary of State in 2005, she became the highest-ranking woman in the United States presidential line of succession in history until **Nancy Pelosi** was elected Speaker of the House the following year. Barack Obama appointed **Hillary Clinton** as his first Secretary of State and a total of eight women to Cabinet positions, the most of any Presidency, surpassing George W. Bush's record of six, though no cabinet has had more than four women serving simultaneously.

Frances Perkins (1880-1965) by Arlene Holmes © 2016
First Woman Cabinet Member in the U.S. Government and the Woman Behind the New Deal

*"I had more sense of obligation to do it for the sake of other women than I did for almost any other one thing.
It might be that the door would close on them and that weaker women wouldn't have a chance."*

Zitkala-Ša (1876–1938) "Red Bird" also known by the missionary-given name Gertrude Simmons Bonnin
Yankton Dakota Sioux Writer, Musician, Teacher and Native American Activist

Born in the year of the Battle of the Little Bighorn, Zitkala-Ša spent the first eight years of her life with her mother on the Yankton Indian Reservation in South Dakota –a time she later described as happy and free among her people. When she was eight, she was taken away to a missionary boarding school in Indiana for "poor children, white, colored, and Indian." In her autobiography **The School Days of an Indian Girl** she later contrasted the misery of having her heritage stripped away, having to pray as a Quaker and cut her traditionally long hair, and even losing her own tribal name with the joy of learning to read and write and to play the violin. Returning to Yankton at age 11, Zitkala-Ša realized she was now torn between two worlds – still feeling the pull of her Sioux traditions but seeing that many there were adopting white ways.

At age fifteen, Zitkala-Ša returned to the school to continue her studies and teach piano and violin. She delivered the graduation speech on women's inequality and received high praise from the local paper. Though her mother wanted her to return home, Zitkala-Ša received a scholarship and enrolled in Earlham College in Indiana. University education for women was very unusual at the time and almost unheard of for a Native American. Overcoming her sense of isolation among the mostly white student body, she soon became a well-known speaker on campus. Wanting to preserve her heritage, she started gathering Native American legends, translating them first to Latin and then to English for children to read. After Earlham, she moved to Boston, playing violin with the New England Conservatory of Music from 1897 to 1899 then becoming a music teacher at the Carlisle Indian Industrial School in Pennsylvania. She brought the band to the Paris Exposition of 1900, but when she returned to the Yankton Reservation to recruit students, she discovered her family had fallen into poverty, and that white settlers were occupying Yankton Dakota lands.

On her return to Carlisle, she published an article in **Harper's Monthly** describing the profound loss of identity felt by a Native American boy after undergoing the assimilation enforced at the school – and was fired. She returned to Yankton to care for her mother and began collecting and writing stories from Native Americans which she published in **Old Indian Legends.** She also took a job at the Bureau of Indian Affairs (BIA) and met and married Captain Bonnin, a mixed-race man with one-quarter Yankton Dakota ancestry. The BIA sent them to the Uintah-Ouray reservation in Utah. There Zitkala-Ša became active in the Society of American Indians (SAI). After she criticized the BIA's policy of prohibiting Native American children from using their native languages and cultural practices at the national boarding schools and forcing them to say Christian prayers, the BIA dismissed her husband. They moved to Washington D.C. and she began lecturing across the country on behalf of the SAI to promote the cultural and tribal identity of Native Americans. In 1926, she and her husband founded the National Council of American Indians, whose mission was to unite the tribes throughout the U.S. to seek full citizenship rights through suffrage. Zitkala-Ša also persuaded The General Federation of Women's Clubs (a grassroots organization dedicated to promoting women as "municipal housekeepers") to form their Indian Welfare Committee. She co-wrote **Oklahoma's Poor Rich Indians: An Orgy of Graft and Exploitation of the Five Civilized Tribes - Legalized Robbery** exposing corporations which had robbed and even murdered Native Americans in Oklahoma to gain access to their lands. This led to the passage of the Indian Reorganization Act of 1934 (sometimes called the "Indian New Deal.") which enabled tribes to restore and adopt self-government and returned the management of their lands to Native Americans. Zitkala-Ša continued to work for civil rights, better access to health care and education for Native Americans until her death in 1938. The crater "Bonnin" on Venus is named in her honor.

Read More – *for Teens and Adults:* **Old Indian Legends**, 1901 and the autobiographical **American Indian Stories, 1921, Oklahoma's Poor Rich Indians: An Orgy of Grant and Exploitation of the Five Civilized Tribes - Legalized Robbery**, 1924 – all by Zitkala-Ša . **Red Bird, Red Power: The Life and Legacy of Zitkala-Ša** by Tadeusz Lewandowski, 2016.

Visit: Arlington National Cemetery Arlington, VA Zitkala-Ša is buried under the name Gertrude Simmons Bonnin.
Smithsonian National Museum of the American Indian New York NY and Washington DC www.nmai.si.edu

Zitkala-Ša (1876–1938) "Red Bird" (also known by the missionary-given name Gertrude Simmons Bonnin)
Yankton Dakota Sioux Writer, Musician, Teacher and Native American Activist
by Julie Goetz © 2016

"the voice of the Great Spirit is heard in the twittering of birds, the rippling of mighty waters,
and the sweet breathing of flowers"

Fascinating Factoid: In addition to her works chronicling her identity struggles between the majority culture and her Native American heritage and her books retelling traditional Native American stories, Zitkala-Ša collaborated with American composer William F. Hanson to write the libretto and songs for *The Sun Dance Opera,* the first American Indian opera. It was based on a sacred Sioux ritual, which the federal government had prohibited the Ute from performing on the reservation. When the opera premiered in Utah in 1913, featuring both Ute and non-native performers, it received widespread local praise.

Elouise Pepion Cobell (1945-2011) Yellow Bird Woman
Tribal Activist who Worked to Restore Funds Owed to Native Americans
Banker, rancher, and lead plaintiff in the groundbreaking class-action suit *Cobell v. Salazar*

"We were treated like nobodies, even though it was our own money."

Decades after Zitkala-Ša's death, Native American tribes were still being exploited by the government and corporations leasing their lands until one woman decided to ask the right questions – and refused to take "no" for an answer. Elouise Pepion grew up in the 1950s on her parents' cattle ranch on the Blackfeet Reservation in Montana. Like many reservation families, they did not have electricity or indoor plumbing. After graduating from a one room school, going to high school, business college and taking business classes at Montana State University, she became treasurer for the Blackfeet Nation and wondered why tribal members were receiving practically nothing (literally pennies a month) from the oil and gas extraction and ranching on tribal land.

In 1887, Congress had passed the General Allotment Act ending tribal collective ownership and dividing Indian reservations into individual allotments. Then, declaring allottees were "incompetent" to manage their own lands, the Department of the Interior (DOI), leased the allotments for grazing or mineral extraction. Although it had leased millions of acres of Indian-owned land for nearly a century, the DOI failed to document how much money was made, where that money went, or that the Indian landowners were paid. When Elouise and other tribal members wrote the Bureau of Indian Affairs (BIA), they replied that she was "not capable" of understanding basic accounting and refused to provide documentation. But Elouise persisted and, after over a decade of government rebuffs, she sued. In 1996 Elouise, represented by Dennis Gingold (renowned banking lawyer) and with financial support from the Native American Rights Fund, became lead plaintiff in *Cobell v. Salazar* – a class action suit against the BIA and DOI on behalf of half a million American Indians for mismanagement of trust funds. It demanded the payment to individual Indians of the money—perhaps as much as $127 billion dollars—that was rightfully theirs. The Justice Department fought back. It spent over $30 million on teams of lawyers from 35 prestigious American law firms and destroyed hundreds of boxes containing tens of thousands of documents in defiance of a court order. But Elouise and her team of lawyers persisted. When she won a MacArthur "genius" award of $310,000 for her work exposing government corruption, she donated much of the money to support the continuing lawsuit. Finally, in 2009, after 13 years of fighting and nine lost appeals, then Secretary of the Interior Ken Salazar agreed to settle the case and President Barack Obama signed the Claims Resolution Act. The $3.4 billion settlement is the largest in U.S. history, but far less than the hundreds of billions of dollars actually owed Indian landowners. Elouise remarked, *"Although we have reached a settlement totaling more than $3.4 billion, there is little doubt this is significantly less than the full accounting to which individual Indians are entitled. Yes, we could prolong our struggle and fight longer, and perhaps one day we would know, down to the penny, how much individual Indians are owed. Perhaps we could even litigate long enough to increase the settlement amount. But we are compelled to settle now by the sobering realization that our class grows smaller each year, each month and every day, as our elders die and are forever prevented from receiving their just compensation."*

In addition to serving as the treasurer of the Blackfeet Nation, Elouise was a tribal elder, rancher and banker. She founded the first Native American owned bank in the country and later became Director of the Native American Community Development Corporation. The Blackfeet honored her with warrior status in 2002. *"Elouise will always be remembered . . . as a woman who fought the battle many of us didn't know how to fight."* Elouise died of cancer in 2011, but her courage and tenacity continue to inspire American Indians who fight against government usurpation of Indian lands most recently in the 2016 standoff by the Standing Rock Sioux against the Dakota Access Pipeline. In 2016, she was awarded a Presidential Medal of Freedom by President Obama.

Fascinating Factoid: Elouise also served for a time as president of Montana's Elvis Presley fan club. During her funeral procession, the car radios were tuned to Elvis songs.

Learn More – Her story is told in the documentary *100 Years: One Woman's Fight for Justice* (2016) and in obituaries and other articles linked on her Wikipedia page.

Smithsonian National Museum of the American Indian New York NY and Washington DC www.nmai.si.edu

Elouise Pepion Cobell (1945-2011) "Yellow Bird Woman" by Aarti Arora © **2016**
Tribal Activist who Worked to Restore Funds Owed to Native Americans

"This young person was so ignorant to us, it was so bad. He told me, 'We ought to be charging you for the handling of this money.' I almost jumped across the table."

"This is totally unreal. Sometimes I think the department's behavior has deteriorated to the bottom of the basement, and things like this happen, and I think it's gone to the fiery bowels of the earth."

Rosa Parks (1913-2005) "The First Lady of Civil Rights"

*"People always say I didn't give up my seat because I was tired, but that isn't true.
No, the only tired I was, was tired of giving in."*

Many historians date the beginning of the modern civil rights movement in the United States to Thursday, December 1, 1955. That was the day when a 42-year-old seamstress in Montgomery, Alabama refused to give up her bus seat to a white passenger. At the time, buses (and many other places) in the South had separate sections for blacks and whites. Rosa was sitting in the front row of the black section when a white passenger boarded. Because there were no seats left in the white section, the driver ordered her to stand and give up her seat. She refused. The police were called, she was arrested and she spent the night in jail for violating a city ordinance. Her actions were no accident. Rosa, the granddaughter of slaves, had joined the National Association for the Advancement of Colored People (NAACP) in 1943 and was the secretary of the Montgomery chapter. She had also attended workshops by Septima Clark using nonviolent civil disobedience and decided she would "face whatever came" if it advanced the cause of civil rights for African Americans.

On the night of Rosa's arrest, the Women's Political Council led by Professor Jo Ann Robinson, mimeographed 35,000 copies of a flyer announcing a bus boycott for Monday, the day of Rosa's trial. The next morning, a young pastor named Martin Luther King Jr. and other activists held a meeting to plan details of the boycott. Rosa received a standing ovation. The boycott would demand a fixed dividing line for the segregated sections of the buses so that blacks would not be forced to give up their seats to whites. On Sunday, plans for the Montgomery Bus Boycott were announced at local black churches and on the front page of the ***Montgomery Advertiser***. At a church rally that night, those attending agreed unanimously to continue the boycott until they were treated with courtesy, black drivers were hired, and seating in the middle of the bus was handled on a first-come basis. On Monday, Rosa was tried, found guilty and fined $14. Despite heavy rain that day, the black community held their bus boycott. People rode in carpools and traveled in black-operated cabs that charged the same fare as the bus, 10 cents. Many of the 40,000 black commuters walked, some as far as 20 miles.

For over a year, thousands of African Americans refused to ride buses, organizing carpools, bicycling and even walking many miles each day instead. Rosa and her husband were fired from their jobs, but the boycott was featured on the nightly news – and the whole country learned about the boycott and the woman whose actions started it. Finally, after 381 days and a tremendous loss of money (75% of their passengers had been black), the bus company gave in to the boycotters' demands.

The following year, Rosa's case was tried before the Supreme Court and the Court ruled that all segregation in public places was unconstitutional. Rosa's act of defiance began a movement that ended legal segregation in America and made her an inspiration to freedom-loving people everywhere. Rosa, however, continued to receive threats on her life in Alabama, so she and her family moved to Michigan. In 1965, she became an aide to Congressman John Conyers. After her retirement in 1988, she founded the Rosa and Raymond Parks Institute for Self-Development to offer career training to young African Americans. She received many awards for her courage, including the Martin Luther King Jr. Nonviolent Peace Prize in 1980 and the Congressional Gold Medal of Honor in 1999.

Fascinating Factoid: Rosa Parks Day is celebrated in California and Missouri on her birthday (February 4) and on the day she was arrested (December 1) in Ohio and Oregon.

Read More *(a sampling)* *for Kids:* **If a Bus Could Talk** by Faith Ringgold, 1999. **I am Rosa Parks** by Rosa Parks, 1997. **Who Was Rosa Parks?** by Yona Zeldi McDonough, 2010. **Rosa** by Nikki Giovanni, 2005. **Back of the Bus** by Aaron Reynolds, 2010. *for Teens and Adults:* **The Rebellious Life of Mrs. Rosa Parks** by Jeanne Theoharis, 2013.

Visit: Rosa Parks Library and Museum Montgomery, AL www.troy.edu/rosaparks/museum
Smithsonian National Museum of African American History and Culture Washington DC nmaahc.si.edu

Rosa Parks (1913-2005) "The First Lady of Civil Rights"
by Rachel Wintemberg © 2016   thehelpfulartteacher.blogspot.com

" I had not planned to get arrested. I had plenty to do without having to end up in jail. But when I had to face that decision, I didn't hesitate to do so because I felt that we had endured that too long. The more we gave in, the more we complied with that kind of treatment, the more oppressive it became."

Septima Poinsette Clark (1898-1987) "Freedom's Teacher"
Founder of Citizenship Schools to Enable Black Voters to Overcome Voting Barriers

"The only thing that is really worthwhile is change – and it's coming."

Septima's first experience of school as a youngster in Charleston, South Carolina, was sitting on a set of bleachers with a hundred other six-year-olds, learning nothing. Her mother pulled her out and found a woman who was running a private school for girls. Septima babysat the woman's children in exchange for tuition. She went on to attend Avery School, a high school founded by white women missionaries from Massachusetts, and was there when the first black teachers were hired in 1914. This was controversial because at the time Charleston Public Schools prohibited black teachers.

Septima graduated high school in 1916 but couldn't afford college. Instead eighteen-year-old Septima became both teacher and principal of a rural two-room school. She and another teacher taught all 132 students – when they were able to attend. The students, needed in the fields, were often absent. The school had few resources – not even desks and blackboards. *"I wrote their stories...of their country right around them, where they walked to come to school, the things that grew around them...They told them to me, and I wrote them on dry cleaner's bags and tacked them on the wall...It's surprising that I had so many children who became very competent."* For all this, she made $35 a week. In contrast, the teacher in the white school nearby who taught three students made $85. In the evening "Miss Seppie" (as she was called) ran an adult school on her own time, developing innovative teaching methods like using the Sears Catalog to quickly teach them to read and write.

After three years, she returned to Charleston when she was offered a teaching position at her old high school. There she joined the National Association for the Advancement of Colored People (NAACP) and led her students around the city in a petition drive to allow black principals at Avery. It was the first of many actions she would take challenging segregation and the illiteracy that "separate but (un)equal" schools created. In 1956, two years after the Supreme Court school declared segregated schools illegal in "Brown vs. Board of Education," Septima, upset that African American teachers received lower salaries than white ones, petitioned the Charleston Board of Education for better pay. They promptly fired her for this and for being a member of the NAACP and revoked her 30 years of retirement pay.

No other South Carolina school system would hire her, so Septima decided to open her own "citizenship schools." There she taught African Americans to read and write and spell c-o-n-s-t-i-t-u-t-i-o-n so they might pass the "literacy tests" many Southern states had set up to prevent blacks from registering to vote. In 1961, Septima was recruited by Martin Luther King's Southern Christian Leadership Conference (SCLC) to become director of education and teaching. While traveling across the South to recruit new teachers for her "Freedom Schools," Septima refused to sit in the "colored" section. Like fellow activist Ella Baker, Septima worked hard for the civil rights movement but was disappointed that the men did not respect the women in the cause saying it was *"one of the greatest weaknesses of the civil rights movement."* Later in her life, Septima returned to Charleston, and after long legal battles with the State of South Carolina, won her pension and back pay. In 1979, President Carter gave her the Living Legacy Award, and in 1982, South Carolina awarded her the Order of the Palmetto, the state's highest honor of service.

Fascinating Factoid: In 1962, the SCLC along with four other Civil Rights groups joined together to form the Voter Education Project. Over the next four years they trained 10,000 teachers for Citizenship Schools and registered nearly 700,000 African Americans to vote. Septima had a few tricks up her sleeve. Once, when the staff at a voter registration site pretended to be closed because they saw African Americans coming, Septima sent a light-skinned woman ahead. When the site opened for the "white" woman, the rest of the group hurried through the door as well.

Read More – *for Kids:* **Women of Hope** by Joyce Hansen, 1998. *for Teens and Adults:* **Ready from Within: A First Person Narrative** by Septima Clark, 1986. **Freedom's Teacher** by Katherine Mellen Charron, 2009.

Visit: Smithsonian National Museum of African American History and Culture Washington DC nmaahc.si.edu

1898
1987

Septima Poinsette Clark

HIGHLANDER LIBRARY

SITE of EARLY

CITIZENSHIP SCHOOLS

KNOWLEDGE COULD EMPOWER marginalized groups in ways that formal legal equality couldn't

Septima Poinsette Clark (1898-1987) "Freedom's Teacher" by Judy Hnat © 2016 facebook.com/judyhnat.art

"I'd tell the children of the future that they have to stand up for their rights...
they need to come forth and stand up for some of the things that are right."

Ella Baker (1903-1986)
"Unsung Heroine of the Civil Rights Movement"

Ella Baker was raised by her grandparents in a small town in North Carolina. From an early age, she saw community organizing and service modeled by her grandfather – a minister and a respected leader actively helping those in their segregated community. Ella graduated at the top of her class from Shaw University (an all-black college), then moved to Harlem in 1929 just as the Great Depression began. There she started a club to help poor people stretch their resources by sharing what they had. Soon she moved on to broader forms of organizing. She was particularly active in the National Association for the Advancement of Colored People (NAACP) working as field secretary, national director of branches and president of the New York City Chapter. In the 1950s, she helped establish NAACP chapters in the South where she worked with Rosa Parks to establish a chapter in Montgomery Alabama and became a key strategist during the Montgomery bus boycott. By the time Dr. Martin Luther King, Jr. enlisted her help to organize the Southern Christian Leadership Conference (SCLC) in 1957, Ella already had nearly 30 years of civil rights experience.

Ella was the driving force behind many of the SCLC initiatives including the "Crusade for Citizenship" voter registration drives but was never given an official leadership role – likely because she was female. In 1960, when the Student Nonviolent Coordinating Committee (SNCC) was formed and began to organize actions to integrate public places, Ella became a trusted advisor. SNCC members – black and white – sat at "whites only" lunch counters and picketed and boycotted stores and other businesses. She was also a leading voice in the fight to integrate politics, forming the Mississippi Freedom Democratic Party (MFDP) in 1964. (The Mississippi Democratic Party allowed participation only by whites even though African Americans made up 40% of the state population.) The MFDP soon had 60,000 members and it was featured on the national news when it tried to unseat Mississippi's all-white delegation at the Democratic National Convention that year.

In the 1960s and 1970s Ella, along with Fannie Lou Hamer (who had given an impassioned speech at that same 1964 convention), led the effort to register thousands of southern African Americans so that they could actually exercise the vote that had been promised by the 15th and 19th amendments. Over the course of her long life, Ella was an advisor to nearly 50 organizations – not leading but creating leaders who worked for democracy, equality, and justice for all. She spoke out against apartheid in South Africa and allied herself with a number of women's groups, including the Third World Women's Alliance and the Women's International League for Peace and Freedom. She remained an activist until her death in 1986 on her 83rd birthday. Called *"One of the most important African American leaders of the twentieth century and perhaps the most influential woman in the Civil Rights Movement,"* she was honored on a postage stamp in 2009.

Fascinating Factoid: Ella Baker was given the Swahili name *"Fundi"* – a person who passes skills and knowledge to a younger generation. She was critical of charismatic leadership and a fan of grassroots organizing. She believed that ordinary people must get involved in political activity, stating that: *"Strong people do not need strong leaders."*

One of those "ordinary people" was Joan Trumpauer Mullholland, a young white woman who felt compelled to go down South and fight for justice there. Young people can read her inspiring story in **She Stood for Freedom** by Loki Mulholland and Angela Fairwell (2016).

Read More – *for Kids:* **Let in Shine: Stories of Black Women Freedom Fighters** by Andrea Davis Pinkney, 2000. *for Teens and Adults:* **Ella Baker and the Black Freedom Movement: A Radical Democratic Vision,** by Barbara Ransby, 2003. **Stories of Women in the 1960s: Fighting for Freedom** by Cath Senker, 2015.

Visit: Ella Baker Center for Human Rights Oakland, CA ellabakercenter.org
Smithsonian National Museum of African American History and Culture Washington DC nmaahc.si.edu

Ella Baker (1903-1986) "Unsung Heroine of the Civil Rights Movement" by Aarti Arora © 2016

"Until the killing of black men, black mothers' sons, becomes as important to the rest of the country as the killing of a white mother's sons, we who believe in freedom cannot rest until this happens." (1964)

Fannie Lou Hamer (1917-1977)
African American Voting and Civil Rights Activist

Fannie Lou was the 20th child in a sharecropper family. When she was born, the plantation paid her mother $50 – for producing a future field hand. Her grandparents were slaves and her own family, though free, wasn't much better off. They still worked on the same plantation and, though every member of the family worked sunup to sundown, it seemed they could never get ahead. They were "sharecroppers" but their share was never enough to pay the owner's charges for seed, food, clothing and supplies. Fannie Lou started picking cotton at age six to help her family. Though she loved learning, her schooling was sporadic, working cotton always took priority. Fannie Lou was so desperate to learn that she gathered newspaper pages from the roadsides and magazines from the plantation's trash. Her father's plan to get ahead by buying a wagon, plow, three mules and two cows was sabotaged when a white neighbor poisoned their animals. Most of her siblings moved north, but she stayed behind to look after her mother. She married and continued to pick cotton for 20 more years – until the day she tried to register to vote in 1962.

That summer, students from the Student Nonviolent Organizing Committee (SNCC) came looking for volunteers who would go to the courthouse and try to register to vote. At the time, Fannie Lou didn't even know that black people had the right to register to vote –so-called "literacy tests" and high poll taxes meant poor sharecropping families like hers could not vote. But when the SNCC students asked for volunteers, she raised her hand. She later reflected: *"The only thing they could do to me was kill me and it seemed like they'd been trying to do that a little bit at a time since I could remember."* She was the first one into the courthouse. The clerk wrote down her name and workplace, then asked her to read, copy and explain parts of the Mississippi Constitution– then failed her when she could not. On the way home, a policeman stopped the bus and fined them $30 saying it looked too much like a school bus. Furious that African Americans would dare to try to vote, white folks shot bullets at their house and kicked them off the farm.

Out of a home and out of a job, Fannie Lou was still determined to claim her right to vote as a citizen of the United States. She became active in SNCC and the Southern Christian Leadership Conference (SCLC) and, she along with Ella Baker, led a huge voter registration drive and launched the Mississippi Freedom Democratic Party. After she was arrested in 1963 for helping other African Americans register to vote, police officers ordered another prisoner to beat her. Though hurt so badly that one of her hands was permanently crippled, she did not give up. Fannie's speech to the 1964 Democratic Convention Committee about her brutal life as a sharecropper and her prison beating was shown on national TV and it galvanized public opinion. *"If the Freedom Democratic Party is not seated now, I question America."* As a result of her speech, the Democratic Party eventually banned segregated delegations. Her work also led to the passage of the Voting Rights Act in 1965, which eliminated the unfair tests and fees that had prevented many African Americans from voting. In the following years, Fannie became a key women's rights and anti-war activist and joined Betty Friedan, Shirley Chisholm and Gloria Steinem to form the National Women's Political Caucus in 1971. She said, *"We have a job as black women, to support whatever is right."* The fight is not over – in 2013, the Supreme Court gutted a key provision of the 1965 Voting Rights Act that she and others worked so hard to pass. As a result, majority black communities are facing longer lines and other obstacles to voting.

Fascinating Factoid: Beatings and threats did not deter Fannie Lou – deeply religious, she would begin many of her speeches with the spiritual "This Little Light of Mine." She said she wasn't singing for show, she was singing for freedom. Singing was far from safe. Betty Mae Fikes, a teenage member of the Freedom Singers (the music arm of SNCC) spent three weeks in jail in 1963 for singing "This Little Light of Mine" during the Civil Rights demonstrations in Selma.

Read More *for Kids:* **Voice of Freedom: Fannie Lou Hamer, Spirit of the Civil Rights Movement** by Carole Boston Weatherford, 2015 (Caldecott Honor Book). *for Teens and Adults:* **This Little Light of Mine: The Life of Fannie Lou Hamer** by Kay Mills, 2007.

Visit: Fannie Lou Hamer Civil Rights Museum Belzoni, MS www.thefannielouhamercivilrightsmuseum.com

Fannie Lou Hamer (1917-1977) by Kim Wood © 2016 kimwoodstudio.com
African-American Voting and Civil Rights Activist

"I am sick and tired of being sick and tired. We must stand up for our freedom."

"Nobody's free until everybody's free."

Dolores Huerta (1930-) Labor Leader, Women's and Migrant Rights Advocate

"Every moment is an organizing opportunity, every person a potential activist, every minute a chance to change the world."

Growing up during the Great Depression, Dolores was no stranger to hardship. Her parents divorced when she was three and her mother moved the family to Stockton, California to run a hotel and restaurant for migrant workers – allowing them to stay even if they couldn't pay. Dolores also knew discrimination firsthand. In school, Dolores' teacher accused her of cheating – her teacher thought the paper was too well-done to have been written by a Mexican American. When Dolores grew up, she became a teacher in a poor migrant school. Seeing that the children there were too hungry to learn, Dolores became a community activist, joined the Community Service Organization (CSO) and began visiting workers in their homes and on farms, telling them about reading and writing classes and registering those eligible to vote. She worked for laws protecting Hispanic Americans.

In 1956, Dolores met César Chávez, another CSO volunteer. Together they formed the National Farm Workers Association (NFWA) in 1962. In the spring of 1965, the NFWA helped underpaid rose farmers to organize a strike. In less than a week, the grower agreed to pay higher wages. That fall, they joined with another union to create a strike against grape growers – not just for better pay but for protection against pesticide-laden dust from the growers' farm equipment. This time the growers sent in dogs to attack the workers, beat them, called them derogatory names and brought in replacements. In March 1966, César led strikers on a 300 mile march to the capitol of California to publicize the migrants' plight. A week later, one grape grower agreed to increase the workers' pay. Over the next few years, Dolores organized a nationwide grape boycott of non-union-grown grapes. Finally in 1970, the growers agreed to a contract – negotiated by Dolores – that gave the workers higher pay and better protections. When some farmers balked, Dolores lobbied for the passage of the California Agricultural Labor Relations Act (ALRA) to allow unions to organize farm workers.

Since ALRA passed in 1975, Dolores has continued to work for worker's and women's rights – giving speeches across the nation encouraging Latinas to be leaders. In 1998 **Ms.** magazine named Dolores "Woman of the Year" and President Bill Clinton presented her with the U.S. Presidential Eleanor D. Roosevelt Human Rights Award. Today, the Dolores Huerta Foundation trains activists to fight for fair and safe workplaces.

Fascinating Factoid: On June 5, 1968, Dolores was standing beside Robert F. Kennedy as he delivered his victory speech in the California Democratic presidential primary – just minutes before he was shot. Twenty years later, Dolores was severely beaten by San Francisco Police Officers during a peaceful demonstration against the policies of then-candidate for President George H.W. Bush. The video was broadcast widely on local television news. Dolores later won a large judgment against the SFPD and San Francisco, which she donated to be used for the benefit of farm workers. And at age 72, she led workers on a 165-mile-march in 100-degree weather to urge California to support workers' rights.

Another senior citizen who let her walking do her talking was **Doris "Granny D" Haddock** (1910 –2010). A political activist from New Hampshire, 88-year-old "Granny D" set out on January 1, 1999 and walked 3,200 miles across the country to advocate for campaign finance reform before finishing 14 months later. In 2004, at age 94, she ran as a Democrat for the U.S. Senate but lost to incumbent Republican Judd Gregg.

Read More – *for Kids:* **Dolores Huerta: A Hero to Migrant Workers** by Sarah Warren, 2012. **Side by Side/Lado a Lado: The Story of Dolores Huerta and Cesar Chavez** by Monica Brown and Joe Cepeda, 2010. *for Teens and Adults:* **Dolores Huerta: Labor Leader** by Debra A. Miller, 2006.

Visit: No permanent museum exhibit. www.californiamuseum.org/inductee/dolores-huerta.
California Museum Sacramento, CA www.si.edu/Exhibitions/Details/One-Life-Dolores-Huerta-5691

Dolores Huerta (1930-) by Natalie Obedos © 2016 yellowfences@tumblr.com
Labor Leader, Women's and Migrant Rights Advocate

"Every single day we sit down to eat breakfast, lunch, and dinner, and at our table
we have food that was planted, picked, or harvested by a farm worker.
Why is it that the people who do the most sacred work in our nation
are the most oppressed, the most exploited?"

Betty Friedan (1921-2006)
Groundbreaking Author of the 1963 Book *The Feminine Mystique* Which Kicked off a New Wave of Feminism

Betty grew up in Peoria, Illinois, daughter of a mother who had given up a career in journalism to be a housewife. Bright and outgoing, Betty started a literary magazine in high school and graduated class valedictorian, then went to college, studied psychology and became editor of the college newspaper. A feisty journalist, she gained a reputation for her daring editorials. After graduation, she became a labor journalist in New York City and saw firsthand the discrimination women faced in the workplace and in society. Though she gave up her full-time job after she married and had a son, she tried to continue to write freelance pieces – her family needed the money and she loved the intellectual stimulation – but these were few and far between. In 1957, feeling discontented with her own life as a housewife, she polled some of her classmates at her 15th college reunion to find out how they were feeling – and found many felt the same way. Expected to be "happy housewives," many of these bright, college-educated women were anything but – bored and frustrated with their limited and confining lives. Betty wrote an article about her survey, but no magazine would print it. Finally a publisher gave her an advance of $1000 to expand it into a book. Five years and many more interviews later, she published **The Feminine Mystique** describing "the problem that has no name."

Thousands of women immediately recognized themselves in her writing and they realized they were not alone. Betty's book described the frustration of trying to be "the perfect housewife and mother" and kicked off a new wave of feminism. In it, she wrote, *"The feminine mystique says that the highest value and the only commitment for women is the fulfillment of their own femininity"* and that there was *"only one definition [of fulfillment] for American women ...housewife-mother."* It showed how, through social conditioning, women were denied independence, opportunity, and equality with men and it became an instant best-seller. Betty divorced her husband, gave up being a housewife, and became an active speaker and political organizer.

In 1966, she along with Pauli Murray, and other feminists, founded the National Organization for Women (NOW) which soon became the major voice of the women's movement in the United States. Betty became NOW's first president. The following year, Betty, along with Shirley Chisholm, Fannie Lou Hamer, and Gloria Steinem, created the National Women's Political Caucus to bring women and women's concerns into politics. In the 1970s, she helped establish the First Women's Bank and Trust Company (so women could get credit and bank accounts in their own names and control the money they deposited), advocated for abortion rights, worked for government-sponsored child care and the Equal Rights Amendment. Betty continued writing and exploring the roles and expectations for women and families. In 1981, her book **The Second Stage** examined the conflicts women experienced balancing freedom with love and family. Her 1993 title, **The Fountain of Age,** exposed how our society undervalued older people and in 1997 she wrote **Beyond Gender: The New Politics of Work and Family** exploring how society might balance work and family issues.

Fascinating Factoid: The Equal Rights Amendment simply states: *Equality of rights under the law shall not be denied or abridged by the United States or by any state on account of sex.* It was first proposed by suffragist leader Alice Paul in 1923 and finally passed by the Congress in 1972 but was only ratified by 35 states, 3 states short of the 38 required to put it into the Constitution. Over the years, there have been various attempts to revive the amendment, but it is still not a part of our Constitution.

Read More – *for Kids and Teens:* **The Feminist Revolution: A Story of the Three Most Inspiring and Empowering Women in American History: Susan B. Anthony, Margaret Sanger, and Betty Friedan** by Jules Archer and Naomi Wolf, 2015. **Herstory,** ed. by Ruth Ashby, 1995. *for Adults:* **The Feminine Mystique** by Betty Friedan, 1963.

Visit: Place setting at Judy Chicago's *Dinner Party* **Elizabeth A. Sackler Center for Feminist Art** Brooklyn, NY www.brooklynmuseum.org/eascfa/dinner_party

Betty Friedan (1921-2006) by Lena Shiffman © 2016
Feminist Writer and Catalyst for the "Second Wave" of Feminism

"The problem that has no name — which is simply the fact that American women
are kept from growing to their full human capacities — is taking a far greater toll
on the physical and mental health of our country than any known disease."
– The Feminine Mystique, 1963

Gloria Steinem (1934-) Founder of Ms. Magazine
Outspoken Champion for the "Second Wave" of the Women's Rights Movement

"The only alternative to being a feminist is being a masochist."

After a difficult childhood caring for her mentally ill mother, Gloria received a scholarship to attend Smith College and decided to study government, a non-traditional choice for a woman at that time. Graduating with honors, she accepted a fellowship to do research in India. There she was intrigued by the peaceful grassroots organizing principles of Mahatma Gandhi – ideas which she would later apply to her feminist activism in the United States.

In 1960, Gloria moved to New York to pursue a career as a journalist. For several years, she wrote freelance pieces for various publications. Then, in 1963, *Show* magazine hired her to report undercover as a Bunny at the Playboy Club. Her resulting article revealed that, contrary to the glamorous image of the Bunny, the waitresses were actually overworked and underpaid. It was a serious article but it was the "Bunny" image that stuck – editors refused to give Gloria serious stories to write. Finally in 1968, she landed a job as a founding editor at *New York* magazine. There she reported on political campaigns and social issues – including the demands of the new Women's Liberation movement. She attended rallies, protests and sit-ins and became an active speaker for the Equal Rights Amendment, reproductive freedom and other feminist issues. In 1971, Gloria and five other women created *Ms.* – a new magazine devoted to promoting women's rights. It started out as an experimental insert in *New York* magazine – eight days later, all 300,000 copies had sold out! In 1972, *Ms.* was launched as an independent magazine and Gloria became its first editor-in-chief. That same year, she and other "second-wave" feminists including Bella Abzug and Betty Friedan formed the National Women's Political Caucus to recruit, train, and support women seeking elected and appointed offices.

Gloria helped create other organizations and programs including the Women's Action Alliance (which assisted women working on practical, local action projects such as battered women's shelters) and the first "Take Our Daughters to Work Day" in 1993 to show girls and young women employment possibilities. In 1995 *Parenting* magazine selected her for its Lifetime Achievement Award for her work in promoting girls' self-esteem. In 2004, *Biography* magazine listed her as one of the 25 most influential women in America and in 2013, President Obama awarded her the Presidential Medal of Freedom, the nation's highest civilian honor. Gloria continues to work as a writer, lecturer, and political commentator on progressive social issues .

Fascinating Factoid: "Ms." (as a title for women's names that would not indicate whether or not she "belonged" to a man) had been suggested as early as 1901, but rarely used until Sheila Michaels, a 22-year-old civil rights worker in New York City spotted "Ms." on a piece of mail in 1961. She became a passionate advocate for its adoption and in 1971, a friend of Gloria Steinem heard Sheila use it during a radio interview. Feminists loved the idea of a title that didn't indicate marital status and "Ms." became the title of the iconic magazine the following year. The U.S. Government Printing Office authorized its use in federal publications in 1972 but *The New York Times* refused to use it until 1986!

Read More – *for Kids:* **Who is Gloria Steinem?** by Sarah Fabiny, 2014. *for Teens and Adults:* **My Life on the Road** by Gloria Steinem, 2016. **Outrageous Acts and Everyday Rebellions** (2nd ed.) by Gloria Steinem, 1995. **Moving Beyond Words: Age, Rage, Sex, Power, Money, Muscles: Breaking Boundaries of Gender** by Gloria Steinem, 1994. **The Education of a Woman** by Carolyn Heilbrun, 1996. Video: PBS documentary MAKERS www.makers.com/gloria-steinem (2013), a continuing project to record the women who made America.

THE TRUTH WILL SET YOU FREE BUT FIRST IT WILL PISS YOU OFF.

Ms. VOTE
THE GENDER

Gloria Steinem (1934-) Founder of Ms. Magazine by Jill Schmidt © 2016
Outspoken Champion for the "Second Wave" of the Women's Rights Movement
Ms. cover by permission of Ms. magazine, © 2016

"This is no simple reform. It really is a revolution. Sex and race – because they are easy and visible differences –
have been the primary ways of organizing human beings into superior and inferior groups and into the cheap
labor on which this system still depends. We are talking about a society in which there will be no roles other than
those chosen or those earned. We are really talking about humanism."

Marian Wright Edelman (1939-) Founder of the Children's Defense Fund

"Service is the rent we pay for living.
It is the very purpose of life, and not something you do in your spare time."

Marian grew up in segregated Bennettsville, South Carolina where she saw discrimination and grinding poverty all around her. Even though she was the daughter of a respected minister and lived in a house with a grand piano and good library, she couldn't play in the public playgrounds, drink at the water fountain, or buy a soda at a lunch counter – all because she was black. The adults in their community tried to make children feel valued and important – and her father built a playground for the black kids behind his church – but it didn't take away the sting of being considered second class. Marian grew up with a sense of responsibility toward those less fortunate.

When it came time for Marian to go to college in 1956, two years after the Brown vs. Board of Education Supreme Court decision, the question arose: should she try to challenge a white college? Some in the family liked the idea, but her mother was afraid of the possible violence, so Marian went to Spelman College, the largest liberal arts college in the country for black women. On campus, free of racism, the students could focus on academics and leadership skills – but the school also trained its young women to be well-mannered and respectful so that off campus they presented no challenge to Atlanta's culture of white supremacy. At Spelman she met Dr. Howard Zinn, a recent graduate of Columbia University who had been hired to integrate the faculty. Dr. Zinn was a revisionist historian who would later write the best-selling **A People's History of the United States.** Marian – bright, articulate, and confident – had many discussions with this activist professor who inspired his students to try to challenge the segregation all around them. Though they had some modest successes (including the main library), most Atlanta institutions remained segregated.

At the end of her sophomore year, Marian won a scholarship to spend the summer studying at the Sorbonne in Paris. She then moved to the University of Geneva in Switzerland to study international relations. While in Europe, she met people from all around the world in an atmosphere mostly free of the racial constraints she'd known all her life, *"almost like breathing clean air for the first time."* She also found a sense of purpose, writing *"I have seen and felt the suffering of others and gained incentive to alleviate it in my own small way."* Returning to the states, she enrolled in Yale Law School and graduated in 1963. Marian became the first black woman admitted to the Mississippi Bar then took a job at the NAACP (National Association for the Advancement of Colored People) Legal Defense and Educational Fund Mississippi office. She worked on racial justice issues and represented activists during the Mississippi Freedom Summer of 1964 – getting civil-rights protesters out of jail. She also fought for school desegregation and started a Head Start program. There she found her life's work – America's poor children. In 1968, Marian moved to Washington DC and created the Washington Research Project to give legal representation to people of color and those in poverty. In 1973, she founded the Children's Defense Fund (CDF) to advocate for services for poor and minority children. For more than 50 years, Marian has urged America to invest money and resources to protect and aid children. Over the years, she has received dozens of honorary degrees, a MacArthur Fellowship and the Presidential Medal of Freedom. She says the *"legacy I want to leave is a child-care system that says no kid is going to be left alone or unsafe."*

Fascinating Factoid: Hillary Rodham Clinton considers Marian Wright Edelman one of her most important mentors. Ten years after Marian graduated, Hillary also went to Yale Law School and she worked as an intern at the Children's Defense Fund. Hillary's first published paper "Children Under the Law" examined abused and neglected children – "child abuse" was a brand-new field and Hillary was one of the first to study it at the Yale Child Study Center.

Read More – *for Kids and Teens:* **Marian Wright Edelman: The Making of a Crusader** by Beatrice Siegel, 1995.
I Can Make a Difference: A Treasury to Inspire Our Children by Marian Wright Edelman and Barry Moser, 2005.
for Teens and Adults: **The Measure of Our Success: A Letter to My Children and Yours** by Marian Wright Edelman, 1993. **A People's History of the United States** by Howard Zinn, 1980. (also Young People's Edition).

Marian Wright Edelman (1939-) by Sheryl Depp © 2016 primarilyartwithmrsdepp.blogspot.com
Founder of the Children's Defense Fund

"You just need to be a flea against injustice. Enough committed fleas biting strategically can make even the biggest dog uncomfortable and transform even the biggest nation."

"A lot of people are waiting for Martin Luther King or Mahatma Gandhi to come back – but they are gone. We are it. It is up to us. It is up to you."

A Woman's Place is in the House...and the Senate!
The Supreme Court, The State Department
and Tribal Government

- Jeannette Rankin (1880-1973) –"I may be the first woman member of Congress but I won't be the last"

- Patsy Mink (1927-2002) – The First Asian American Woman Elected to Congress

- Bella Abzug (1920-1998) – "Battling Bella" Outspoken Liberal Activist and Politician Who Introduced the First Gay Rights Bill in Congress

- Patricia Schroeder (1940-) – Congresswoman Known for Her Witty and Biting One-Liners

- Barbara Jordan (1936-1996) – Black Congresswoman Who was Called "The Conscience of the Nation"

- Sandra Day O'Connor (1930-) – First Woman Supreme Court Justice

- Ruth Bader Ginsberg (1933-) – "Sister in Law"

- Sonia Sotomayor (1954-) – First Latina Supreme Court Justice

- Madeleine Albright (1937-) – First Woman to Become U.S. Secretary of State "The Most Powerful Woman in the World"

- Wilma Mankiller (1945-2010) – First Woman Chief of the Cherokee Nation

- Nancy Pelosi (1940-) – First Woman to Become Speaker of the House

- Elizabeth Warren (1949-) – Feisty Democratic Senator and Consumer Advocate

Jeannette Rankin (1880-1973)
First Female Member of Congress and Peace Activist

"I may be the first woman member of Congress, but I won't be the last."

Four years before the 19th Amendment gave women across the nation the right to vote, Jeannette Rankin became the first woman member of the United States Congress. Jeannette had graduated from the newly opened University of Montana with a degree in biology but couldn't get a job in that male-only field. So she worked as a teacher, seamstress and social worker where she saw many families living in poverty. She decided that the existing laws kept people poor and that women would change those laws – if only they were allowed to vote. In 1910, Jeannette traveled all over Washington State giving speeches for women's suffrage. When the men's votes were counted (only the men could vote), the referendum passed. In 1914, her speeches helped win women the vote in her home state of Montana. It was time, she decided, for her to run for Congress. Many people thought she was crazy. Most thought she couldn't win. But on November 6, 1916, Jeannette voted for herself and the next day she learned she had won. Newspaper photographers mobbed her house to see the "freak."

On March 5, 1917, she walked into the House of Representatives. That same day, President Woodrow Wilson called for a vote for the U.S. to join Great Britain and France in their war with Germany. Jeannette was a pacifist. She knew that voting against the war would be unpopular, that it would reinforce the stereotype of women being weak and unable to handle big issues like war. She knew it meant she would probably not be re-elected, but when the vote came, she was one of 56 members to vote "Nay." *"I want to stand by my country, but I cannot vote for war."* She did not turn her back on the soldiers – she voted for many military bills so the soldiers fighting would have the best chance of returning home safely. During the rest of her term, she also worked to improve health conditions for women and children, stood up for striking mine workers and spoke out strongly in favor of the 19th Amendment to give women in every state the right to vote.

As she expected, Jeanette lost her 1918 reelection campaign – but she continued to speak out for the causes she believed in. Twenty one years later, with war in Europe and the Great Depression in the U.S., 60-year-old Jeanette successfully ran again for Congress. Again, she tried to keep the U.S. out of war. But on Dec. 7, 1941, Japan attacked Pearl Harbor and on Dec. 8th, President Franklin D. Roosevelt asked Congress to declare war. Only one person in Congress voted against it – Jeannette . *"As a woman I can't go to war...and I refuse to send anyone else."* She received hate mail but she said she could *"bear to be a worm."* After she left congress in 1942, she spent the rest of her life trying to prevent war. In 1967, when she was 87 years old, she led 5000 women in a march on the Capitol to protest the U.S. involvement in the Vietnam War.

Fascinating Factoid: As of 2016, a century after Jeannette began her quest for women's equal representation in Congress, **313** women have served in Congress – vs. **11,864** men. In 2016, there are **104** female members of Congress – **84** in the House and **20** in the Senate – women make up 19.4% of the 535 voting members even though they are 51% of the population. The number of women will remain the same in the new 115th Congress, with 83 in the House and 21 in the Senate. Four of those senators are women of color: Mazie Hirono, the second minority woman ever to serve in the Senate, will be joined by Tammy Duckworth, Kamala Harris, and Catherine Cortez Masto. All are Democrats. The Republican members of Congress remain overwhelmingly white and male. Jeannette also predicted a woman would become president someday, reassuring crowds there would be *"opportunities for boys too. Someday one of you may be the husband of a president."*

Read More – *for Kids and Teens:* **Jeannette Rankin: Political Pioneer** by Gretchen Woelfle, 2007. **Jeannette Rankin: First Lady of Congress** by Trish Marx, 2006. **Jeannette Rankin: Bright Star in the Big Sky** by Mary Barmeyer O'Brien, 2015. **Lives of Extraordinary Women** by Kathleen Krull, 2000. *for Adults:* **Jeannette Rankin, America's Conscience** by Norma Smith, 2002.

Visit: Historical Museum Fort Missoula, MT www.fortmissoulamuseum.org, **Jeannette Rankin Peace Center** jrpc.org

Jeannette Rankin (1880-1973) by Laura Leigh Myers © 2016
First Woman Member of Congress and Peace Activist

I've been trying to help women have better lives, using the laws we already have.
But what if the laws are wrong, or don't go far enough?"

"What one decides to do in a crisis depends on one's philosophy of life,
and that philosophy cannot be changed by an incident...
We are all human beings and we have to live on this earth and
we have to find a way of settling our disputes without force and violence."

Patsy Mink (1927-2002)
First Asian American Woman elected to Congress
(Also the First Asian American Woman to Seek the Presidential Nomination of the Democratic Party)

When Patsy was born on a sugar plantation on the Hawaiian island of Maui in 1927, Hawaii was still a territory of the United States. Patsy's father was the first Japanese American graduate of the University of Hawaii and the first Japanese American civil engineer there – but saw his white colleagues promoted when he was not.

As a child, Patsy listened to President Franklin Delano Roosevelt's "fireside chats" on the radio and decided she too wanted a career in public service. Accordingly, she ran for student body president of her high school – unheard of for a girl! But she had an even greater challenge. A month before the election, Japan bombed Pearl Harbor and Japanese Americans were not popular. Yet Patsy went about building a coalition of various cliques on campus – and won the election.

In 1944, Mink graduated from high school as class valedictorian. She followed her father's footsteps to the University of Hawaii, then transferred to the University of Nebraska, where she initiated a campaign against the injustice of segregated housing. Through letters and speeches, she organized everyone from students to alumni to local businesses – and got the policy reversed. After getting bachelor's degrees in zoology and chemistry, she applied to twenty medical schools – but none would accept a woman. So Patsy decided to go to law school at the University of Chicago so she could fight for women's rights. In 1951, she and her new husband returned to Hawaii and founded the Oahu Young Democrats. Patsy was elected to the Hawaiian House of Representatives in 1957, and in 1959 (the year Hawaii became a state) she won a seat in the Senate. Five years later, she ran and won a seat in the U.S. Congress – her husband was her campaign manager (a reversal of the typical role of woman as assistant).

When Patsy arrived in Congress in 1964, there were only eight women serving – and she was the only woman not of European ancestry and the first Asian American woman in the chamber. She became known as a firecracker and a fighter (contrary to the stereotype of the compliant Japanese female) but also a coalition-builder. She was a liberal activist and an ardent supporter of President Johnson's "great society" civil rights programs. She introduced the first comprehensive Early Childhood Education Act and and transformed America's schools as the co-author of Title IX, a 1972 law which barred discrimination in school programs funded by the federal government and barred sex discrimination in academics, athletics, employment, vocational education, sexual harassment and assault, testing, and much more. (After her death, it was renamed the Patsy T. Mink Equal Opportunity in Education Act.) Patsy was also an impassioned critic of the Vietnam War, which she felt was both unjust and a tragic waste of lives and money. In 1972, she became the first Asian American to seek the presidential nomination of the Democratic Party when she ran in the Oregon primary as an anti-war candidate. Patsy ran for Senate in 1976. After she lost, she returned to Hawaii and worked as a lawyer and university lecturer and stayed active in local Democratic politics. In 1990, she was reelected to the U.S. House of Representatives, where she remained a leader in women's issues, workplace fairness, universal health care, and family and medical leave until her death in 2002.

Fascinating Factoid: During World War II, 110,000 people of Japanese descent in the mainland United States were deported to internment camps on the charge that these people – many of whom were American citizens – were a possible threat to national security. Washington had also planned for the internment of all 158,000 people of Japanese descent living in Hawaii. However, since they made up nearly 40% of the population, this would have been a massive disruption to the island economy, and the wealthy landowners protested. As a result, Hawaii's Japanese American community – including Patsy and her family – were allowed to stay in their homes, schools, and jobs.

Read More – *for Kids and Teens and Adults:* **A Heart in Politics: Jeannette Rankin and Patsy T. Mink (Women Who Dared)** by Sue Davidson, 1994. **A Woman in the House (and the Senate)** by Ilene Cooper, 2014. **Extraordinary Asian Americans and Pacific Islanders** by Susan Sinnott, 2003. DVD: **Patsy Mink - Ahead of the Majority**, 2008

Patsy Mink (1927-2002) by Victoria Ford © 2016
First Asian American Woman Elected to Congress
(Also the First Asian American Woman to Seek the Presidential Nomination of the Democratic Party)

"It is easy enough to vote right and be consistently with the majority . . .
but it is more often more important to be ahead of the majority and this means being willing
to cut the first furrow in the ground and stand alone for a while if necessary."

Bella Savitsky Abzug (1920-1998) "Battling Bella"
Outspoken Liberal Activist and Politician Who Introduced the First Gay Rights Bill in Congress in 1975

"This woman's place is in the House–the House of Representatives"

"We are bringing women into politics to change the nature of politics...
Women are not wedded to the policies of the past. We didn't craft them. They didn't let us."

Bella Abzug spent much of her life fighting for social and political change. The daughter of Russian immigrants, Bella grew up in the Bronx, New York, where her father ran a butcher shop. In the 1930's, she decided she wanted to be a lawyer – a rare occupation for a woman at that time. She was elected president of the student council at Hunter College, then earned her law degree from Columbia University in 1947 (since Harvard wouldn't accept women). Bella started out as a labor lawyer then became a lawyer for the American Civil Liberties Union. She defended Willie McGee, a black man convicted of raping a white woman in Mississippi. He was sentenced to death, but many were not convinced of his guilt. Bella faced numerous threats from white supremacists for her involvement in the case. Bella also defended many people who had been accused of communist activities by Senator Joseph McCarthy.

In the 1960s, Bella worked in the antinuclear and peace movements. She was one of the organizers of the Women's Strike for Peace in 1961. To promote women's issues and to lobby for reform, she helped establish the National Women's Political Caucus with leading feminists Betty Friedan and Gloria Steinem. Deciding she needed to be inside the political process to advance her causes, Bella ran for Congress in 1970, declaring *"This woman's place is in the House–the House of Representatives"* in her successful campaign. She took office in 1971 and made a bold move on her first day in Congress – introducing a bill to remove all U.S. troops from Vietnam. Though the bill failed, it was just the first of many bills by Bella.

Bella ran for the U.S. Senate in 1976 but was narrowly defeated by Daniel Patrick Moynihan. The next year she ran for mayor of New York City, but lost to Ed Koch in the primaries. President Gerald Ford appointed her to chair the 1977 National Women's Conference and, in 1978, President Jimmy Carter appointed her to co-chair the National Advisory Committee for Women – but dismissed the outspoken Bella the following year. Bella tried again for public office in 1986, running for Congress from New York's Westchester County, but she lost out to her Republican opponent. While public office eluded her, she continued to work on many causes in the 1980s and 1990s. She established the Women's Environmental Development Organization and traveled to China in 1995 for the United Nations Fourth World Conference on Women. When she died in 1998, her onetime opponent Ed Koch, said of this great political powerhouse, *"The women of the world, not just the country, owe her a great debt. She stood up for them as nobody else. She was their champion."* Today the Bella Abzug Leadership Institute trains young women to become the leaders of tomorrow.

Fascinating Factoid: Bella – nicknamed "Battling Bella" – was often criticized for her bold statements. She fought tirelessly for women's rights and for civil rights in general. In 1975, Bella made history when she introduced the first gay rights bill in Congress. One of Washington's most colorful characters, she was noted for her flamboyant hats. She remarked, *"I began wearing hats as a young lawyer because it helped me to establish my professional identity. Before that, whenever I was at a meeting, someone would ask me to get coffee. "*

Read More – *for Kids and Teens:* **Is There a Woman in the House – or Senate?** by Bryna J. Fireside, 1994. **Portraits of Jewish American Heroes** by Malka Drucker, 2008. *for Adults:* **Bella Abzug: How One Tough Broad from the Bronx Fought Jim Crow and Joe McCarthy, Pissed Off Jimmy Carter, Battled for the Rights of Women and Workers, Railed against War and for the Planet, and Shook Up Politics Along the Way** by Suzanne Braun Levine, 2007. **Bella!: Ms. Abzug goes to Washington** by Bella S Abzug, 1972. **Gender Gap: Bella Abzug's Guide to Political Power for American Women** by Bella S Abzug, 1984.

Visit: Bella Abzug Leadership Institute New York, NY   www.abzuginstitute.org

Bella Savitsky Abzug (1920-1998) "Battling Bella" by Justine Turnbull © 2016

"We are coming down from our pedestal and up from the laundry room."

*"Our struggle today is not to have a female Einstein get appointed as an assistant professor.
It is for a woman schlemiel to get as quickly promoted as a male schlemiel."*

Patricia Schroeder (1940-) Congresswoman Known for Her Witty and Biting One-Liners

*"When people ask me why I am running as a woman, I always answer, 'What choice do I have?'...
Nobody ever says to men, how can you be a Congressman and a father?"*

Born into a military family that moved from post-to-post, Pat grew up in Texas, Ohio, and Iowa. She earned a pilot's license and operated her own flying service to pay for tuition at the University of Minnesota. When she arrived at Harvard Law School as one of 15 women in the class of more than 500, the dean told the women in the class he did not want them there. Undeterred, Pat stayed and earned her law degree in 1964. Afterwards, she moved out to Denver with her husband and worked as a lawyer for the federal government.

In 1972, with the encouragement of her husband, Pat entered the congressional race as the Democratic Candidate. The local paper announced "Denver Housewife Runs for Congress." It was a grassroots campaign with an average contribution of $7.50 but Colorado voters liked her antiwar and women's rights message and she won 52% of the vote. Pat Schroeder became the first woman elected to Congress from Colorado – but getting to Washington was only half the battle. As a 32-year-old mother with two young children, Schroeder received endless questions about how she could be both a mother and member of Congress. Known for witty and biting one-liners, her memorable retort was: *"I have a brain, I have a uterus, and they both work."*

When Pat was elected to Congress in 1973, the place oozed discrimination. Earlier women in Congress, although they were few (or perhaps because they were few) were treated politely. But in the 1970s, as women started demanding their rights, many men got mean. She was mocked for wearing pants rather than a skirt or dress. She was told she should be at home taking care of her two young sons rather than having a political career. She was refused admission at a Congressional awards dinner because it was being held at the Touchdown Club – an all-male establishment. And when she and Ron Dellums, an African American Representative, were appointed to the Armed Services Committee, the Chairman made them share one chair, saying *"women and blacks were worth only half of one regular member"* and deserved only half a seat. None of the other members of the committee objected nor did they offer to get another chair. But Pat stayed on and became an active member of the committee where she worked to reduce sexual harassment in the armed services.

She would go on to win 11 more elections, typically garnering more than 60% of the vote and with little opposition. She was a force to be reckoned with. She cofounded the Congressional Women's Caucus and she worked on arms control and many liberal issues. Knowing how difficult it was to juggle work and family life, Pat worked particularly hard to get Congress to pass the Family and Medical Leave Act – finally a parent could take up to 12 weeks of unpaid leave to care for an ill family member without risking losing their job. She was also an advocate for transparency in government, saying *"Government has become a machine that runs only when gold coins are inserted..I had always believed government was not a fungus: It could survive in sunshine."* Pat stayed in Congress until 1996, continuing to work passionately for legislation to help women and families. Afterwards, she became a Princeton University professor and president and CEO of the Association of American Publishers.

Fascinating Factoid: Pat Schroeder coined the famous phrase "Teflon President" to describe Ronald Reagan. She says she was frying eggs in a Teflon pan one morning when the idea came to her.

Read more – *for Teens and Adults*: **24 Years of Housework...and the Place Is Still a Mess: My Life in Politics** by Pat Schroeder, 1998. **Champion of the Great American Family** by Patricia Schroeder, 1989. **Video:** www.makers.com/pat-schroeder

Visit: Capitol Hill Washington DC www.visitthecapitol.gov

*"When men talk about defense, they always claim to be protecting women and children,
but they never ask the women and children what they think."*

Patricia Schroeder (1940-) by Kim Wood © 2016 kimwoodstudio.com
Ground-breaking Congresswoman Known for Her Witty and Biting One-Liners

"The Pledge of Allegiance says "...with liberty and justice for all." What part of "all" don't you understand?"

"Our tax code encourages people to raise thoroughbred horses, not children."

If you want to change the world, you change the world of a child."

Barbara Jordan (1936-1996)   African-American Congresswoman and "The Conscience of the Nation"

Barbara Jordan often said *"If you're going to play the game properly you'd better know every rule."*
In her 30 years as lawyer, legislator, teacher and public speaker,
she learned the rules – then fought to change them!

Barbara grew up in a poor black neighborhood in Houston at a time when segregation was the norm and she was expected to ride in the "colored" section of the bus. Her father was a Baptist minister and she was encouraged by her parents to strive for academic excellence. She soon demonstrated a gift for language and building arguments – she was an award-winning debater and orator in high school and the star of Texas Southern University's debate team. After graduation, she enrolled at Boston University Law School – one of two women (both, interestingly, African American) in a class of 600 students. After getting her law degree in 1959, Barbara returned to Texas to practice law. She campaigned for the 1960 Democratic presidential ticket of John F. Kennedy and fellow Texan Lyndon B. Johnson and, as she put it, was *"bitten by the political bug."* In 1962, Barbara decided to run for office herself seeking a spot in the Texas legislature. Two runs failed, but in 1966 on her third try, she won election to the Texas State Senate – and made history as its first woman member. Though initially dismissed and even scorned by some of her colleagues, Senator Jordan was a powerful and convincing public speaker. She got Texas' first minimum wage law passed, worked to create the Texas Fair Employment Practices Commission which outlawed race discrimination in hiring for any state-funded jobs, and worked for environmental laws. In 1972, her fellow lawmakers voted her president pro tempore of the state senate – the first African American woman to hold this post.

In 1972, the year Shirley Chisholm ran for president, Barbara Jordan was elected as the first African American congresswoman from the deep South. In Congress, she wrote a bill that outlawed racial discrimination in schools and at companies receiving federal funds. The following year, the new Congresswoman became famous when millions heard her speak on national television during the impeachment trial of President Nixon. As a member of the House Judiciary Committee, she urged the impeachment of the President for his involvement in the illegal political scheme that came to be known as Watergate, saying *"I am not going to sit here and be an idle spectator to the diminution, the subversion, the destruction of the Constitution."* Later, at the 1976 Democratic convention, Barbara Jordan gave the keynote address – one of the most powerful speeches in American history. She asked American citizens, women and men, of all races and religions to come together in a national community: *"My presence here ... is one additional bit of evidence that the American dream need not forever be deferred...We must define the 'common good' and begin again to shape a common future. Let each person do his or her part. If one citizen is unwilling to participate, all of us are going to suffer. For the American idea, though it is shared by all of us, is realized in each one of us."*

Senator Jordan was diagnosed with multiple sclerosis in 1973 and left Congress in 1979. She continued working as a professor in Texas and in 1994 she was appointed Chair of the U.S. Commission on Immigration Reform. That same year, she was awarded the Presidential Medal of Freedom. When she died in 1996, Former Texas governor Ann Richards stated, *"There was simply something about her that made you proud to be a part of the country that produced her."* President Clinton remarked, *"Barbara always stirred our national conscience."*

Fascinating Factoid: Barbara attended an all-black high school and college. Not until she began law school in Boston did she understand just how "separate but equal" had denied her the education her white classmates had received.

Read more – *for Kids and Teens:* **Barbara Jordan** by Rose J. Blue, 1989. *for Adults:* **Barbara Jordan: Speaking the Truth with Eloquent Thunder** edited by Max Sherman, 2007. **CD: We Rise: Speeches by Inspirational Black Women** by Michelle Obama and Shirley Chisholm, 2010.

Visit: Barbara Jordan Archives, Texas Southern University
www.tsu.edu/academics/robert_j_terry_library/specialcollections.php

Barbara Jordan (1936-1996) by Sheryl Depp © 2016 primarilyartwithmrsdepp.blogspot.com
African-American Congresswoman and "The Conscience of the Nation"

"Earlier today, we heard the beginning of the Preamble to the Constitution of the United States:
'We, the People.' It's a very eloquent beginning. But when that document was completed
on the seventeenth of September in 1787, I was not included in that 'We, the People.'
I felt somehow for many years that George Washington and Alexander Hamilton just left me out by mistake.
But through the process of amendment, interpretation, and court decision,
I have finally been included in 'We, the People.'"
— Barbara Jordan, a member of the House Judiciary Committee, during Richard Nixon's impeachment hearing

Sandra Day O'Connor (1930-) First Woman Supreme Court Justice

"I happily share the honor with millions of American women of yesterday and today."
– Sandra Day O'Connor in 1981 on becoming the first woman ever appointed to the U.S .Supreme Court
102 years after Belva Lockwood first won women the right to argue before that court

Born in Texas, Sandra spent much of her childhood on her family's Arizona cattle ranch – often atop a horse managing cows. After graduating from Stanford University in 1950 with a bachelor's degree in economics, she went on to the university's law school and received her degree in 1952. She graduated third in her class of 102 but could not find a single law firm willing to hire a woman lawyer – though one offered to hire her as a legal secretary! She offered to work without pay for the county attorney of California's San Mateo region and soon was promoted to the paid position of deputy county attorney. After a stint working as a civilian lawyer in Frankfurt, Germany, she moved back to Arizona and worked in private practice before being appointed Arizona state assistant attorney general from 1965 to 1969. That year, the governor appointed her to the state senate to fill a vacancy. A conservative Republican, Sandra won reelection twice, then in 1974, she ran and won the position of judge in the Maricopa County Superior Court. Judge O'Connor gained the reputation for being firm but just. In 1979, she was selected to serve on the Arizona Court of Appeals. Two years later, Republican President Ronald Reagan nominated her for the Supreme Court and on September 22,1981, the U.S. Senate voted 99-0 to confirm her – the first woman appointee to that Court in 191 years.

Calling herself FWOTSC (First Woman on the Supreme Court), Justice O'Connor gained a reputation as a strong independent vote. During much of her term the court was evenly split between liberal and conservative justices, so for 24 years, she often cast deciding votes. A moderate conservative, her votes often lined up with the Republican platform, but sometimes broke from its ideology. Her decisions were based on the letter of law – what she believed best fit the intentions of the U.S. Constitution. In 1982, she wrote the majority opinion in *Mississippi University for Women v. Hogan*, when the court ruled 5-4 that a state's formerly all-female nursing school had to admit men. In opposition to the Republican attempt to reverse the *Roe v. Wade* decision legalizing abortion rights in 1992, she provided the vote needed in *Planned Parenthood v. Casey* – breaking away from the dissents penned by fellow conservatives William Rehnquist and Antonin Scalia. In 1999, she sided with the majority opinion in the sexual harassment case *Davis v. Monroe County Board of Education* that ruled that a school board was responsible for protecting a fifth-grade student from unwanted advances from another student. She also cast the deciding vote on the controversial *Bush v. Gore* case in 2000 which ended the recount of votes and gave George W. Bush the presidency. She later admitted that perhaps the highest court should not have weighed in on the election.

After retiring in 2006 to take care of her ailing husband, she launched iCivics, an online civics program aimed at middle school students, saying, *"We have a complex system of government. You have to teach it to every generation."* She continued to speak out on judicial issues. She defended Chief Justice John Roberts for his vote to uphold President Barack Obama's healthcare law against the wishes of fellow conservatives by saying that justices were not obligated to follow the politics of the president who appointed him or her. She also campaigned to end electing judges, believing that having judges run political campaigns compromises the judicial process. President Obama honored her with the Presidential Medal of Freedom in 2009.

Fascinating Factoid: After Sandra Day O'Connor's appointment, the honorific address for Supreme Court members was changed from "Mr. Justice" to "Justice."

Read more – *for Kids:* **Out of Order: Stories From the History of the Supreme Court** by Sandra Day O'Connor, 2013. *for Teens and Adults:* **The Majesty of the Law: Reflections of a Supreme Court Justice** by Sandra Day O'Connor, 2003. **Sandra Day O'Connor: How the First Woman on the Supreme Court Became Its Most Influential Justice** by Joan Biskupic, 2006. **Sisters in Law: How Sandra Day O'Connor and Ruth Bader Ginsburg Went to the Supreme Court and Changed the World** by Linda Hirshman, 2015.

Visit: The Supreme Court Washington DC www.supremecourt.gov/visiting/visiting.aspx

Sandra Day O'Connor by Lynnor Bontigao © 2016 www.lynnorbontigao.com
First Woman Supreme Court Justice

"Looking back, I have to say that selection [as first woman Supreme Court Justice] was a turning point in the history of opportunities for women in the workplace. It opened doors."

Ruth Bader Ginsberg (1933-) "Sister in Law"

"The greatest figures of the American judiciary have been independent thinking individuals with open but not empty minds – individuals willing to listen and to learn."

Ruth was born in Brooklyn and grew up in an immigrant neighborhood of Russian and Eastern European Jews. Anti-Semitism was common. As a girl, Ruth read signs on stores that said "No Jews Allowed " while Hitler was creating the Holocaust on the other side of the Atlantic Ocean. Ruth's mother, Celia, had dreamed of college but her parents felt education was wasted on girls. Instead she had worked long hours in a garment factory – and her wages paid her brother's college tuition! Deciding her daughter would have the education she was denied, Celia saved her own money to make sure it would be possible. Sadly, she died of cancer the night before Ruth's high school graduation.

Ruth enrolled at Cornell on full scholarship and she graduated near the top of her class in 1954. She planned to go to Harvard Law School (which had been all male until 1950) where her new husband was already a student but, when he was drafted, she became an army wife at a base in Oklahoma. It was hard to pay bills on a soldier's salary, so she looked for a job. Even though she had a top degree from Cornell, the only job on base available for women was clerk-typist. To add insult to injury, when her boss found she was pregnant, he demoted her. After the army stint was over, both Ruth and her husband attended Harvard Law School – though Ruth's father urged her to consider a more "sensible" career as a teacher. She was one of nine women in a class of 400. When her husband graduated and got a job in New York City, Ruth had to transfer to Columbia. She acquired the nickname "Ruthless Ruthie" for her hard work, was invited to serve on the staff of both the Harvard and Columbia Law Reviews, and tied for first in class when she graduated in 1959. Ruth wanted to be a law clerk for a justice on the U.S. Supreme Court – a natural aspiration for the top graduate of a top law school – but when the Dean of Harvard Law recommended her to Justice Felix Frankfurter, he said simply *"I don't hire women"* adding *"Does she wear skirts? I can't stand girls in pants."* Judges on lower courts and law firms also refused to hire her. She sent out dozens of applications but received only two interviews and no job offers. Ruth knew why – *"To be a woman, a Jew and mother to boot, that combination was a bit much."* She finally got a job – as a legal secretary!

Ruth learned firsthand about sex discrimination and became determined to fight it. Even textbooks were demeaning. One on property law stated, "*...land, like woman, was meant to be possessed."* She eventually found a job as a clerk for a federal judge in New York City, then returned to Columbia and wrote two books on Swedish law before becoming a professor at Rutgers School of Law in 1963. Ruth rose to full professor in 1969 – an extraordinarily short amount of time – especially since she took a short leave to give birth to her second child in 1965 (she wore baggy clothes to hide her pregnancy since the law school could have fired her). In 1966, the National Organization for Women (NOW) was founded. One of the issues NOW championed was equal pay for equal work. Ruth knew this issue personally because she had discovered that Rutgers was paying female professors less than men. Her experiences made her the perfect lawyer for American Civil Liberties Union (ACLU) sex discrimination cases. From 1973-76, she argued six women's rights cases before the Supreme Court – and won five – including one allowing pregnant schoolteachers to keep their jobs. In 1972, Ruth also became Columbia Law School's first female full professor and the first to get tenure. In 1980 President Carter appointed Ruth to the Court of Appeals where she worked on abortion rights, gay and lesbian rights, and affirmative action for 13 years until President Clinton nominated her to be the second woman on the Supreme Court. Millions watched her confirmation hearings on TV and heard her thoughtful answers to the senators' questions. Because of her reputation for even-handedness, she was easily confirmed by Congress: 96-3 . Ruth joined the dissenting opinion in the 2000 Supreme Court ruling which halted presidential vote recounting in Florida.

Read More *for Kids:* **I Dissent: Ruth Bader Ginsburg Makes Her Mark** by Debbie Levy, 2016. **The Ruth Bader Ginsburg Coloring Book** by Tom F. O'Leary, 2016. *for Teens and Adults:* **Notorious RBG: The Life and Times of Ruth Bader Ginsburg** by Irin Carmon and Shana Knizhnik , 2015. **My Own Words** by Ruth Bader Ginsburg, 2016. **Sisters in Law** by Linda Hirshman, 2015. **Free to Be Ruth Bader Ginsburg: The Story of Women and Law** by Teri Kanefield, 2016.

Visit: The Supreme Court Washington DC www.supremecourt.gov/visiting/visiting.aspx

Ruth Bader Ginsberg (1933-) "Sister in Law" by Jill Obrig © 2016

"Do you realize that you are simply taking the place of a qualified man?"
– Dean of the Law School at Harvard to Ruth Bader Ginsburg and the eight other women accepted into Harvard

"I have a last thank-you. It is to my mother, Celia Amster Bader, the bravest and strongest person I have known, who was taken from me much too soon. I pray that I may be all that she would have been had lived in an age when women could aspire and achieve and daughters are cherished as much as sons."
– Ruth Bader Ginsburg speaking in the White House Rose Garden on her nomination to the Supreme Court 1993

Sonia Sotomayor (1954-) First Latina Supreme Court Justice

Sonia had a tough childhood. She grew up in a public housing project in the New York City neighborhood of the Bronx, the child of two Puerto Rican parents. Because her father was an alcoholic and her mother worked long hours, she spent most of her time at her grandmother's home who, thankfully, gave her warmth and love. At age seven, she was diagnosed with diabetes, and she soon learned how to give herself insulin shots since her mom was often not home and her father's hands trembled. Sonia's father died when she was nine. Sonia's mother insisted that her two children work hard at education, and Sonia and her brother spent many hours studying at the local public library. By age ten, Sonia decided she wanted to become a lawyer when she grew up so she could use her brainpower and the law to right wrongs. This was reinforced when, at age thirteen, she watched the idealistic lawyer and national hero Robert F. Kennedy running for President. In high school, Sonia joined the debate team and graduated at the top of her class. A friend urged her to try for an Ivy League school. Sonia was doubtful – these prestigious colleges were mostly male and very expensive – but she applied to Princeton and received a full scholarship.

Princeton in 1972 was a shock. There were few students from her socio-economic background, few women and few other Hispanic students. There were no Hispanic professors. She had also never been out of a city (and was scared by the sound of crickets!) Classes were tough. Too embarrassed to ask questions, she struggled by herself, studying in the library, but gradually she gained confidence and became an advocate for Puerto Rican students. Princeton's president started seeking Sonia's advice on Hispanic issues and she graduated with highest honors. To fulfill her dream, she needed to go to law school. Yale Law School admitted her with a full scholarship but she was again the outsider – almost all her classmates were wealthy white males. Again she persevered. A professor called her *"extremely warm and very tough...an unusually brainy student "* but she was also condemned by some people for arguing *"like a man."*

After graduation, Sonia had a tough time getting a job. Many firms didn't want to interview a Hispanic-American or a woman but the New York District Attorney's Office was eager to hire her. So Sonia returned to New York City, working from 7 a.m. to 10 p.m., handling up to a hundred cases a day putting criminals behind bars. She moved on to a private law firm that was prosecuting counterfeiters. The job could be dangerous – sometimes she wore a bulletproof vest and once she actually rode on a police motorcycle as they chased down the criminals. In time she was made a partner in the firm – unusual for a woman – and she started to hear rumors that she might be appointed as a judge. In 1992, she was confirmed as a New York federal district judge. She was only 38 years old – the first Latina and the youngest judge in the state. In 1998, she was confirmed to the Court of Appeals. For the next eleven years, she judged thousands of cases and gained a reputation for tough probing questions. On May 26, 2009, Sonia's cell phone rang. President Obama called to tell her she was his first choice to fill the vacancy on the Supreme Court. That July, a Senate Committee grilled her with questions for four days – they were especially concerned about a comment she had once made: *"I would hope that a wise Latina woman with the richness of her experiences would more often...reach a better conclusion that a white male who hasn't lived that life."* Sonia explained that she was only saying that she had lived through poverty and prejudice and that gave her a broader perspective than perhaps other judges had. This time the Senate was more divided, but she was confirmed – 68 for and 31 against – and Sonia Sotomayor became the third woman and first Hispanic Supreme Court Justice in the United States of America.

Fascinating Factoid: Sonia was admitted to Princeton in part because affirmative action made up for her slightly lower standardized test scores. She would later praise affirmative action for creating *"the conditions whereby students from disadvantaged backgrounds could be brought to the starting line of a race many were unaware was even being run."* Fellow Princeton graduate, Elena Kagan became the 4th female Supreme Court Justice in 2010.

Read More – *for Kids:* **Sonia Sotomayor: I'll Be the Judge of That!** by Kathleen Krull, 2015. **Sonia Sotomayor: A Judge Grows in the Bronx / La Juez que Crecio en el Bronx** by Jonah Winter and Edel Rodriguez, 2009. *for Teens and Adults:* **My Beloved World** by Sonia Sotomayor, 2012. **Sonia Sotomayor: The True American Dream** by Antonia Felix, 2011.

Sonia Sotomayor (1954-) First Latina Supreme Court Justice by Aileen Wu © 2016

"Experience has taught me that you cannot value dreams according to the odds of their coming true. Their real value is in stirring within us the will to aspire."

"I strive never to forget the real world consequences of my decisions on individuals, businesses and government."

"Whether born from experience or inherent physiological or cultural differences, our gender and national origins may and will make a difference in our judging."

Madeleine Albright (1937-)
First Woman to Become U.S. Secretary of State, the Nation's Chief Diplomat
"The Most Powerful Woman in the World"

Madeleine was born with the name Marie Jana Korbel in Czechoslovakia two years before the country was invaded by the Nazis at the start of World War II. Her family fled to England, returned briefly to Czechoslovakia after the war and then, when the Communists came to power, moved to the United States. Madeleine was raised Catholic but would later learn that her parents had converted from Judaism and that three of her grandparents died in concentration camps during the Holocaust. In the United States, Madeleine's father, Josef, who had been a journalist and a diplomat, became a professor at the University of Denver. Madeline and one of his favorite students – the future Secretary of State Condoleezza Rice – would learn much about foreign affairs from him.

At college, Madeleine discovered a passion for publishing and politics. In 1976, she was hired to work for President Jimmy Carter's National Security Council. She soon became one of the Democratic party's leading advisors on matters of foreign policy. In 1993, President Bill Clinton appointed her to be the U.S. Ambassador to the United Nations and four years later he nominated her to be Secretary of State. After being unanimously confirmed by a U.S. Senate vote of 99–0, she became the 64th Secretary of State and the first woman to ever hold that position.

She quickly lived up to her reputation as a strong-willed and outspoken problem-solver. As the chief advisor to the President on foreign relations and the nation's chief diplomat, she was called *"the most powerful woman in the world."* She spoke with many foreign leaders – and they were expected to deal respectfully with her. She advocated for increased human rights and democracy, helped negotiate the Oslo peace accords between the Israelis and Palestinians and fought to halt the spread of nuclear weapons from former Soviet countries. (It didn't hurt that she spoke five languages and had a degree in Russian studies!) In 2001, Madeleine received the Heinz Award for Greatest Public Service by an Elected or Appointed Official. Since then, she has continued to serve as a top Democratic advisor on foreign affairs and has remarked, *"I hope I'm wrong, but I'm afraid that Iraq is going to turn out to be the greatest disaster in American foreign policy – worse than Vietnam."*

Madeleine Albright's appointment apparently broke the glass ceiling in the State Department. President George W. Bush appointed **Condoleezza Rice (1954-)** to the position in 2005. Condoleezza, a noted political science professor and accomplished pianist, became the first female African-American Secretary of State. She had grown up in segregated America but her parents had inspired her to dream high: *"My parents had me absolutely convinced that you may not be able to have a hamburger at Woolworth's but you can be President of the United States."* Hillary Clinton became President Obama's first Secretary of State in 2009.

Fascinating Factoid: Madeleine Albright had a collection of over 200 pins which she wore to make statements on her diplomatic travels. Her book **Read My Pins: Stories from a Diplomat's Jewel Box** contains interesting and often humorous stories about jewelry and her diplomatic career and her "Read My Pins" collection is currently touring museums around the country.

Read More *for Kids*: **Madeleine Albright** by Judy Hasday (1999) *for Teens and Adults*: **Madam Secretary: A Memoir** by Madeleine Albright (2012). **Madeleine Albright: Against All Odds** by Michael Dobbs (2000). **What I Told My Daughter: Lessons for Leaders on Raising the Next Generation of Empowered Women** by Nina Tassler (2016).

Visit: Read My Pins: The Madeleine Albright Collection– on tour.

"I wonder," wrote Eleanor Roosevelt, *"whether we have decided to hide behind neutrality?"*
"It is safe, perhaps, but I am not always sure it is right to be safe. . . . Every time a nation which has known freedom loses it, other free nations lose something, too." — Madeleine K. Albright in her book **Prague Winter**

Madeleine Albright (1937-) by Leslie Simon © 2016
First Woman to Become U.S. Secretary of State, the Nation's Chief Diplomat
"The Most Powerful Woman in the World"

"Because of my background, I grew up always interested in foreign policy.
And when I was in whatever school I moved to, I would always start a foreign relations club
and make myself president. But...I never, ever dreamt that I could be Secretary of State.
And it's not that I was particularly modest, but that I had never seen a Secretary of State in a skirt."

"It took me quite a long time to develop a voice, and now that I have it, I am not going to be silent."

Wilma Mankiller (1945-2010)
First Woman Elected Chief of the Cherokee Nation

"I want to be remembered as the person who helped us restore faith in ourselves."

Wilma was born in Oklahoma, one of 11 children in a family living on a farm without indoor plumbing or electricity – so poor that they sometimes wore clothes made from flour sacks and survived by bartering with neighbors. In 1956, when she was 11 years old, the US government strongly urged the Cherokee to relocate into cities and her father moved the family to San Francisco. There they discovered TVs, toilets, bicycles and elevators along with signs in restaurants and stores that said "No dogs. No Indians." Wilma felt lost and angry. She married at age 17 and soon had two daughters. She taught them to read and dance and laugh but wasn't quite sure what to do with herself. She decided to return to school and to college, but she still felt out of place. Then in 1969, a group of Native American students took over the abandoned Alcatraz Island *"in the name of Indians of all tribes."* They wanted to call attention to 500 years of white mistreatment. For next 19 months, Wilma and four of her siblings joined in the protests there. Wilma was energized, and discovered she was a natural-born leader. When her Ecuadorian husband objected to her activities (and her decision to buy, without his permission, a car to get around in), she divorced him. She moved back to Oklahoma, married a Cherokee, helped other tribe members get a university education, and became a vocal activist for the rights of the Cherokee Nation.

Her fundraising and program ideas intrigued Ross Swimmer, the Chief of the Cherokee Nation, who made her his Deputy Chief – a position that had never before been held by a woman. When one of the council members tried to shout her down, she had his microphone turned off so he would have to talk quietly with her. Two years later, when he accepted the job as head of the National Bureau of Indian Affairs, Wilma became Acting Chief. She was responsible for 140,000 people, supervised 1,200 employees and had an annual budget of $75 million. She endured disrespect and hostility, received hate mail, and her property was vandalized, but she persisted. Wilma agonized about whether to run for Chief in 1987 fearing her chances were slim – but she ran and she won – becoming the first woman elected Chief of a tribe in modern times. Chief Mankiller was re-elected in 1991 in landslide victory. During her time as Chief, Wilma founded the Cherokee Nation Community Development Department to help her people could build up their own communities. Wilma persisted in being an exuberant optimist despite many illnesses and severe injuries from a car accident. She encouraged young people to enter public service, take risks, and *"dance along the edge of the roof "* and she encouraged young women to take on leadership roles. ***Ms.*** Magazine named her 1987 "Woman of the Year."

Fascinating Factoids: Women have led other Native nations in earlier times. After the husband of **Nanye-hi** (aka Nancy Ward) (c1738-1822) was killed in battle, she led the Cherokee to victory over Creek warriors. Known as "Beloved Woman," she headed a group of women elders and was a member of the governing council of chiefs. She helped negotiate peace agreements with European settlers and expressed surprise that no white women were on the negotiating team.

Hawaii had a woman chief as well. After Ka'ahumanu's first husband died in 1819, she became co-ruler of Hawaii with the new king. Six feet tall and 300 pounds, **Ka'ahumanu** (1795-1831) literally stood up for the rights of women against many of the tribe's religious taboos – including the prohibition of women eating with men. After learning to read and write from Protestant missionaries, she established schools for all Hawaiians. She continued to actively govern the island, including establishing Hawaii's first code of laws, until her death.

Read More – *for Kids:* **Lives of Extraordinary Women** by Kathleen Krull, 2000. **They Did What? 50 Unbelievable Women and their Fascinating (and True!) Stories** by Saundra Mitchell, 2016. *for Teens and Adults:* **Mankiller: A Chief and Her People** by Wilma Mankiller and Michael Wallis, 2000. **Every Day Is a Good Day: Reflections by Contemporary Indigenous Women** by Wilma Mankiller and Gloria Steinem, 2011.

Chief Wilma Mankiller (1945-2010) by Caroline Yorke © 2016   carolineyorke.com
First Woman Elected Chief of the Cherokee Nation

"I was raised in a household where no one ever said to me,
'You can't do this because you're a woman, Indian, or poor.' No one told me there were limitations.
Of course, I would not have listened to them if they had tried."

Nancy Pelosi (1940-)
First Woman to become Speaker of the House

"[In] over 200 years of our history,
no woman has ever risen to these heights in the Congress of the United States.
No woman has gone to the White House...in a senior position in the Congress
to sit at the table with the President, to discuss the issues facing our country..."

Nancy was the sixth child and first girl in a close knit Italian American family living in Baltimore, MD. Her father had been a Democratic Representative in Congress during the Great Depression and was an ardent supporter of Franklin Delano Roosevelt's New Deal – he even named his second son Roosevelt! In 1947, he became Mayor of Baltimore. Nancy's mother met her father when both were attending law school. Typical of the time, she left school to marry but stayed active helping with her husband's political campaigns and the Democratic Women's Club. Growing up with her mayor father, Nancy decided she wanted to enter public service too, a career choice that was reinforced when, at age 17, she met John F. Kennedy. A few years later Nancy would attend his presidential inauguration.

Nancy studied political science at Trinity College in Washington D.C., then married, moved to New York City and started a family. In 1969, they moved to San Francisco where Nancy became involved as a volunteer in Democratic Politics while raising five children. Once they were grown, she decided to jump into professional politics. In 1987, Nancy ran her first political campaign for a seat in the U.S. House of Representatives – and won. She won again two years later...and again...and again. From the beginning, she was a passionate and articulate supporter of environmental legislation, funding for HIV/AIDS, access to medical care for everyone, and a woman's right to abortion (even though she was Catholic). These stands did not make her popular with Republicans but fellow Democrats liked and respected her. They elected her minority whip in 2001– the first time a woman held this position. In 2002, Nancy achieved another first for women when the Democrats elected her House minority leader –the highest ranking woman in Congress and the highest ranking woman in the political history of the United States. In the 2006 election, the Democrats won a majority of the seats in Congress, and Nancy was chosen by the members of her party as the very first female Speaker of the House of Representatives. As Speaker, Nancy held the most important position in the House of Representatives – she presided over the chamber, appointed committee chairs and members, set the agenda (so she could advance her priorities – including bills on education, health care, and the environment) and signed bills. She was also third in line to the Presidency (after the President and Vice President).

Fascinating Factoid: California has been a leader for women in politics. In 1992, something extraordinary happened – four women won their race for Senator and the Senate suddenly had six women at the same time (the most ever – though they were still a tiny minority compared to the 94 men). Two of those new senators, **Barbara Boxer (1940-)** and **Dianne Feinstein (1933-)**, were from California. Barbara and Dianne have now served in the Senate for nearly a quarter-century. Both have been strong advocates for causes they believe in: Barbara for families, children, consumers and the environment; Dianne on gun control, anti-terrorism, and appropriations (how congress spends taxpayers' money).

Read More – *for Kids:* **Nancy Pelosi** by Amie Jane Leavitt, 2008. **Nancy Pelosi: First Woman Speaker of the House** by Lisa Tucker McElroy, 2008. *for Teens and Adults:* **Know Your Power: A Message to America's Daughters** by Nancy Pelosi and Amy Hill Hearth, 2009. **Madam Speaker: Nancy Pelosi's Life, Times, and Rise to Power** by Marc Sandalow, 2008.

Visit: U.S. Capitol Washington DC www.visitthecapitol.gov

Nancy Pelosi (1940-) by KIm Wood © 2016 kimwoodstudio.com
First Woman to become Speaker of the House

"I accept this gavel in the spirit of partnership. It is a moment for which we [women] have waited over 200 years. Never losing faith, we waited through many years of struggle to achieve our rights. We worked to redeem the promise of America, that all men and women are created equal. For our daughters and our granddaughters, today we have broken the marble ceiling." – Nancy Pelosi on becoming Speaker of the House

Elizabeth Warren (1949-) Feisty Democratic Senator and Consumer Advocate

"Americans are fighters. We're tough, resourceful and creative, and if we have the chance to fight on a level playing field, where everyone pays a fair share and everyone has a real shot, then no one - no one can stop us."

Born in Oklahoma, Elizabeth spent most of her early life on what she referred to as *"the ragged edge of the middle class"* after her father suffered a heart attack that created massive medical bills and prevented him from working. Elizabeth's mother tried to keep the family afloat by working at Sears but the family lost their house and car. When she was 13, Elizabeth began waiting tables at her aunt's Mexican restaurant to help with the family finances, but money was always tight – and a visit to the doctor could be a financial disaster.

Elizabeth was a brilliant student and became a state debate champion. She graduated high school at age 16 and enrolled at George Washington University on a full debate scholarship but left after two years to marry her high school sweetheart, a NASA mathematician. His job took them to Texas and Elizabeth finally finished her degree in speech pathology at the University of Houston at age 26. They moved to New Jersey where Elizabeth worked briefly helping children with disabilities before becoming pregnant. When her first child turned two, she headed to law school at Rutgers University. She got her law degree in 1976, then set up a law office in her home. In 1978, Elizabeth and her husband were divorced.

Elizabeth began researching the economic consequences of the 1978 law making it easier for companies and individuals to declare bankruptcy and discovered that most bankruptcies were middle class families who had had a major illness, job loss, or divorce that had decimated their finances. She remarried in 1980 to another law professor, and they both moved from job to job for more than a decade before finally finding dual law professorships at Harvard in 1995. That year, Elizabeth was asked to advise the new National Bankruptcy Review Commission. She argued strongly against Congressional efforts to limit consumers' ability to file for bankruptcy but, despite her testimony, a very harsh bill passed in 2005 – a victory for the business lobby. In 2008, she was appointed to chair the Congressional Oversight Panel which was created to monitor the $700 billion bank bailout effort known as the Troubled Asset Relief Program. Her investigations and televised public hearings demanding accountability from bank officers and government officials brought her widespread attention. *The Boston Globe* named her "Bostonian of the Year" in 2009. The next year, President Barack Obama appointed her Special Advisor to the Secretary of the Treasury on the Consumer Financial Protection Bureau. Its goal was to police credit lenders and prevent consumers from unwittingly signing up for risky loans but, due largely to Republican opposition, she was not chosen to head the agency.

On September 14, 2011, Elizabeth Warren officially announced her candidacy for U.S. Senate, running against Republican incumbent Scott Brown. A speech she made went viral on YouTube: *"You built a factory and it turned into something terrific or a great idea–God bless! Keep a big hunk of it. But part of the underlying social contract is you take a hunk of that and pay it forward for the next kid who comes along."* Elizabeth won the election in November 2012 – the first woman senator ever elected from Massachusetts. She told her constituents: *"I won't just be your senator, I will also be your champion."* She has sponsored many pieces of legislation, particularly regarding financial transparency and fairness for families. She has also been very critical of the Republicans' refusal to have hearings on the U.S. Supreme Court vacancy created by the death of Antonin Scalia in February 2016, tweeting *"I can't find a clause in the Constitution that says '...except when there's a year left in the term of a Democratic President.'"* On July 25, 2016, she delivered the keynote address on the first night of the Democratic National Convention, the third woman in history (along with Texas Representative Barbara Jordan and Texas Governor Ann Richards) to be given this prestigious speaking position. *"We're here because our choice is Hillary Clinton,"* she said. *"I'm with her."*

Read More – *for Teens and Adults:* **A Fighting Chance** by Elizabeth Warren, 2014. **The Two-Income Trap: Why Middle-Class Parents Are (Still) Going Broke** by Elizabeth Warren, 2016.

Visit: Capitol Hill Washington DC www.visitthecapitol.gov

Elizabeth Warren (1949-) by Aditi Tandon © 2016 www.TwoDotts.com
Feisty Democratic Senator and Consumer Advocate

"People have hearts, they have kids, they get jobs, they get sick, they cry, they dance.
They live, they love, and they die. And that matters."

The Road to the White House:

- **Victoria Woodhull (1838-1937)** – First Woman to Run for President of the United States

- **Belva Lockwood (1830-1917)** – First Woman Lawyer to Argue before the Supreme Court, Second Woman to Run for President

- **Edith Bolling Wilson (1872-1961)** – Rumored to be Acting President of the United States

- **Eleanor Roosevelt (1884-1962)** – First Lady to the World and Champion of Human Rights

- **Margaret Chase Smith (1897-1995)** – First Female Senator Elected in Her Own Right and the First Woman to Seek the Nomination of a Major Political Party (Republican)

- **Lady Bird Johnson (1912-2007)** – Environmentalist and Activist First Lady

- **Shirley Chisholm (1924-2005)** – First Black Congresswoman and First African American Woman to Run for President

- **Rosalynn Carter (1927-)** – "More a Political Partner than a Political Wife"

- **Geraldine Ferraro (1935-2011)** – First Female Vice Presidential Candidate from a Major American Political Party

- **Hillary Rodham Clinton (1947-)** – First Woman Nominee for President from a Major Political Party

Victoria Woodhull (1838-1937)
First Woman to Run for President of the United States

"There is something wrong with a government that makes women the legal property of their husbands. The whole system needs changing, but men will never make the changes. They have too much to lose."

In 1872, women still didn't have the right to vote – and wouldn't get that right for another 48 years. But that year Victoria Woodhull, journalist and co-owner (with her sister) of the first woman-owned stock brokerage in the United States, ran as a candidate for President.

Born to an illiterate mother and a petty criminal father, with only three years of elementary school education, Victoria married an alcoholic at age 15 and soon became a mother to a disabled son. With such challenges, Victoria would have seemed to be an unlikely person to seek the highest office in the land. Her rise came in an equally unlikely form – fortune-telling. After the Civil War, Victoria and her sister, Tennessee, worked as clairvoyants in New York City. One of their clients was railroad baron Cornelius Vanderbilt. The stock tips they received from him netted the sisters $700,000 during the 1869 gold panic. With this financial backing, Victoria and Tennessee then opened their own highly-publicized Wall Street firm – Woodhull, Claflin & Co. – and became the first female stockbrokers on Wall Street. However, they were unable to get a seat on the New York Stock Exchange – no woman would break into that male bastion until 1967.

Victoria attended a female suffrage convention in January 1869 and immediately became an ardent activist. She spoke before the U.S. House Judiciary Committee arguing that the recently enacted 14th and 15th amendments actually gave women the vote since some women (like her) paid taxes – *"the citizen who is taxed should also have a voice in the subject matter of taxation"* – but the committee rejected her petition to pass the necessary legislation. In April 1870, two months after opening her brokerage firm, Victoria announced her candidacy for president of the United States – campaigning on a platform that included women's suffrage, regulation of monopolies, an eight-hour workday, abolition of the death penalty and welfare for the poor. She promoted herself in her own weekly newspaper and organized the Equal Rights Party, which nominated her at its May 1872 convention. The famed African American abolitionist Frederick Douglass was selected as her vice-presidential running mate (though apparently without his permission – since he campaigned for incumbent President Ulysses S. Grant). Her name appeared on ballots in at least some states but no one knows how many votes she received because many were thrown away by the male electors. She received no electoral votes.

Fascinating Factoid: Victoria spent election day in jail. She and her sister were arrested for libel after their newspaper published articles exposing the misbehaviors toward women of popular preacher Henry Ward Beecher and a wall street trader. The sisters were later acquitted but they remained very unpopular in the press. In 1877, she and Tennessee moved to England – though she returned to run for president in 1892.

Read More – *for Kids:* **A Woman for President: The Story of Victoria Woodhull** by Kathleen Krull, 2004.
for Teens and Adults: **The Woman Who Ran For President** by Lois Beachy Underhill and Gloria Steinem, 1995.
Notorious Victoria by Mary Gabriel, 1998). **The Scarlet Sisters: Sex, Suffrage, and Scandal in the Gilded Age** by Myra MacPherson, 2014. DVD: **America's Victoria: Remembering Victoria Woodhull** (1998).

Visit: Museum of American Finance New York, NY moaf.org/exhibits/women_of_wall_street

Victoria Woodhull (1838-1937) by Arlene Holmes © 2016
First Woman to Run for President

"I now announce myself as candidate for the Presidency. I anticipate criticism;
but however unfavorable I trust that my sincerity will not be called into question."

Belva Lockwood (1830-1917)
First Woman Lawyer to Argue before the Supreme Court, Second Woman to Run for President

"There is something wrong with a government that makes women the legal property of their husbands. The whole system needs changing, but men will never make the changes. They have too much to lose."

In 1869, Belva Lockwood decided she wanted to be a lawyer. She sent applications to many law schools but all refused her admission. Columbia Law School said she *"would distract the attention of the young men."* Finally Belva received an acceptance from the new National University Law School in Washington D.C. But after Belva and another woman finished the coursework in 1873, the law school refused to give them diplomas – so she wrote the president:

To His Excellency U.S. Grant, President U.S.A. – Sir - You are, or you are not, President of the National University Law School. If you are its President, I desire to say to you that I have passed through the curriculum of study in this school, and am entitled to, and demand, my diploma. If you are not its President, then I ask that you take your name from its papers, and not hold out to the world to be what you are not." – Very Respectfully, Belva A. Lockwood

And she got her diploma, signed by the president! In 1876, Belva attempted to argue a case before the U.S. Supreme Court but they refused to hear her because she was a woman. She lobbied Congress for three years until they passed a bill that she had written which would allow any female lawyer with a good reputation and three years' practice in state supreme courts to go before the Supreme Court. In 1879, Belva became the first woman lawyer to argue a case there. One of her cases extended that same right to African-American lawyers. She also won $5,000,000 for the Eastern Cherokee in their suit against the government after the Federal Government forced them off their lands.

Belva was an active suffragist and public speaker. She supported Victoria Woodhull's candidacy for President in 1872. In 1880 and 1884, Belva tried to convince the Republican Convention to include women's suffrage in their platform. When they refused, she tried another tactic. She said, *"I cannot vote – but I can be voted for."* And in 1884, the Women's National Equal-Rights Convention nominated Belva as their presidential candidate. Belva and her running mate Marietta Stow traveled across the country campaigning, raising money, giving speeches, and printing the ballots that would be required in each municipality. Newspapers and critics mocked her campaign – some men even donned dresses and created "Belva Lockwood Parades." Sadly, her candidacy also caused a rift in the women's rights groups. The National Woman Suffrage Association refused to support her. But Belva continued to insist that all Americans deserved equal rights – and she got some support in surprising places. *The Washington Evening Star* wrote *"it is evident that Mrs. Lockwood, if elected, will have a policy...that will commend itself to all people of common sense."* Belva didn't win – but she did win more than 4,711 *male* votes – no one knows how many because, in many municipalities, votes were thrown away or given to other candidates. In response, Belva petitioned Congress to regulate ballots and oversee polling places to prevent voter irregularities but she was ignored. She ran again in 1888. All her life, she continued actively promoting women's suffrage but died in 1917, three years before it was achieved.

Fascinating Factoid: Belva was the first woman to ride around Washington, D.C. on a tricycle – a variation on the new widely-popular bicycle. She rode around the city speeding at up to ten miles per hour! Her transport attracted attention and so many women followed suit that *The New York Times* wrote, *"Now a woman on a tricycle attracts no more attention than a woman on a horse."*

Read More– *for Kids:* **Ballots for Belva** by Sudipta Bardhan-Qaullen, Abrams, 2008. *for Teens and Adults:* **Belva Lockwood: The Woman Who Would Be President** by Jill Norgren, 2007.

Visit: The U.S. Supreme Court Washington D.D. www.supremecourt.gov/visiting/visitorservices.aspx

Belva Lockwood (1830-1917) by Arlene Holmes © 2016
First Woman Lawyer to Argue before the Supreme Court, Second Woman to Run for President

"Why not nominate women for the important places?
It is quite time we had our own party, our own platform and our own nominees.
We shall never have equal rights until we take them, nor respect until we command it."
– Belva Lockwood's letter in **The Woman's Herald of Industry.**

Edith Bolling Wilson (1872-1961)   Presidentress?

Edith Bolling was a 42-year-old widow when she met 58-year-old President Woodrow Wilson in 1915. His wife had died the year before and he was a lonely man, dealing with his own grief and the worries of a Great War in Europe. Each was attracted to the other's personality and intelligence and they exchanged frequent letters. Those letters spoke of more than their love for each other – Edith wrote: *"Much as I enjoy your delicious love letters I believe I enjoy even more the ones in which you tell me what you are working on...then I feel I am sharing your work and being taken into partnership..."*

In May 1915, German submarines sank the British passenger ship Lusitania, drowning 128 Americans. President Wilson wrote a protest letter to Germany. When he showed it to Edith, she suggested that he make it even stronger, and he did. On December 18, 1915 they were married. When he ran for reelection the following year, Edith was at his side at many campaign events. However, she couldn't vote for him – women wouldn't get the vote for four more years.

On October 2, 1918, President Woodrow Wilson suffered a severe stroke. Edith Bolling Wilson became the gatekeeper to her husband – no one saw the President without her permission, and most didn't see him at all. All his responses to questions by Congress and Cabinet Ministers were written in Edith's handwriting and began with the words *"The President says..."* Though she claimed that she *"never made a single decision"* without the President's approval , how much the President actually said and how much was Edith's alone is a hotly debated subject. Some medical records suggest that he was sometimes incapable of understanding or speaking his mind. If that is indeed the case, Edith's actions were a clear violation of the Constitution (which says that in the case of a President's death or incapacitating illness, the Vice President should take over the President's duties). It would also mean that Edith was, in essence, the first female President of the United States. Indeed, Senator Henry Cabot Lodge labeled her *"the Presidentress who had fulfilled the dream of the suffragettes by changing her title from First Lady to Acting First Man."*

Fascinating Factoid: Edith Wilson became "Presidentress" a year before the 19th Amendment granted women the right to vote. Eighty-eight years later Hillary Clinton famously said, as she conceded the 2008 Democratic Party nomination to Barack Obama, *"We didn't shatter the glass ceiling, but we put eighteen million cracks in it."* Sean Munger notes that *"She may have been right, but she forgets that there are a few smudges on that ceiling that bear Edith Wilson's fingerprints as well."*

Read More – *for Children and Teens:* **Edith Wilson: the Woman Who Ran the United States** by James Cross Giblin, 1992. *for Adults:* **Ellen and Edith: Woodrow Wilson's First Ladies** by Kristie Miller, 2010. **Madam President: The Secret Presidency of Edith Wilson** by William Hazelgrove, 2016.

Visit: Edith Bolling Wilson Birthplace Museum, Wytheville, VA. www.edithbollingwilson.org
Woodrow Wilson Presidential Library and Museum, Staunton, VA. www. woodrowwilson.org

Edith Bolling Wilson (1872-1961) by Jen Wistuba © 2016 WordPlayPortraits.com

"I studied every paper, sent from the different Secretaries or Senators,
and tried to digest and present...the things that...had to go to the President."

Eleanor Roosevelt (1884-1962)   First Lady to the World and Champion of Human Rights

"'No one can make you feel inferior without your consent. Never give it."

"Do something every day that scares you."

Ten years after Woodrow and Edith Wilson left office, the nation had another trailblazing First Lady. Eleanor had a tough childhood. Her mother died when she was eight, her alcoholic father two years later. She was called ugly by her grandmother who gave her little love or affection and sent her to boarding school in England at age 15. But there she got lucky. A teacher recognized promise in this lonely, fearful young woman and encouraged her to study languages and literature and volunteer in needy communities. When she returned to the United States, she met and married Franklin Delano Roosevelt (FDR), a distant cousin and ambitious politician. FDR was paralyzed by polio in 1921 but eventually returned to politics and won the presidential election of 1932 in the midst of the Great Depression. Millions of people were out of work and out of hope. Eleanor became her husband's eyes, ears, hands, and feet on the ground. Down-to-earth and approachable, she visited prisons, coal mines, and mental hospitals. She traveled around the country speaking with dust bowl farmers, tenant farmers and factory workers. She listened to their hardships and then encouraged her husband to act on what she found. Eleanor was completely unpretentious. She cared nothing for clothes or cooking and once served hot dogs to the King and Queen of England!

An incredibly hard worker, Eleanor was the first First Lady to write her own daily newspaper column, deliver a weekly radio address and hold her own press conferences – encouraging women journalists. She passionately advocated for the poor and underprivileged and for the advancement of women in society and in government. It was at least partially due to her urging that President Roosevelt appointed the first woman Cabinet Secretary, Francis Perkins, as Secretary of Labor. *"I was weary of reminding him to remind the members of his cabinet and his advisors that women were in existence, that they were a factor in the life of the nation..."* During World War II, she fought (unsuccessfully) for the U.S. to admit more European Jewish refugees and she urged fair treatment of Japanese Americans.

After her husband died in 1945, Eleanor became a delegate to the United Nations and advocated passionately for them to adopt the Universal Declaration of Human Rights. Eleanor left the UN in 1953 but continued traveling and speaking all over the world to promote world peace. She also stayed active in the United States, particularly encouraging more jobs for women. Upon her death, one of her supporters said, *"She would rather light a candle than curse the darkness...and her glow warmed the world."*

Fascinating Factoid: Eleanor was a staunch advocate for the rights of African Americans. Once while attending a conference in the South, she was told that blacks and whites were not permitted to sit in the same sections of the auditorium. When informed by a police officer that she was breaking the law when she tried to sit in the section with the blacks, she picked up her chair and sat in the middle of the aisle!
After the Daughters of the American Revolution refused to let the great African American opera singer Marian Anderson perform in their concert hall, Eleanor tried to get them to change their policy. When they refused, she quit the organization, invited Marian to sing at the White House for the King and Queen of England and arranged an outdoor concert at the Lincoln Memorial. On Easter Sunday, 75,000 people came to hear Marian sing.

Read More: (There are dozens of biographies of Eleanor – here are just a few favorites) *For Kids:* **Eleanor, Quiet No More** by Doreen Rappaport , 2009. **Eleanor Roosevelt: A Life of Discovery** by Russell Freedman, 1997. **Who Was Eleanor Roosevelt?** by Gare Thompson, 2004. **Amelia and Eleanor Go For a Ride** by Pam Munoz Ryan, 1999. *for Teens and Adults:* **Our Eleanor: A Scrapbook Look at Eleanor Roosevelt's Remarkable Life** by Candace Fleming, 2005. **No Ordinary Time: Franklin and Eleanor Roosevelt: The Home Front in World War II** by Doris Kearns Goodwin, 1995. **The Autobiography of Eleanor Roosevelt** by Eleanor Roosevelt (many editions).

Visit: Val-Kill Cottage – Eleanor Roosevelt National Historic Site. Hyde Park, New York, www.nps.gov/elro/index.htm

Eleanor Roosevelt (1884-1962) "First Lady to the World" by Arlene Holmes © 2016

"Every woman in public life needs to develop skin as tough as a rhinoceros hide."

"Where, after all, do universal rights begin? In small places, close to home...in the world of the individual person...where every man, woman, and child seeks equal justice, equal opportunity, and equal dignity, without discrimination." – Eleanor Roosevelt in a speech to the UN

Margaret Chase Smith (1897-1995) First Female Senator Elected in her Own Right*
First woman to Run for President from a Major Political Party

In 1940 when Republican U. S. Representative Clyde Smith became very ill, he asked his wife, Margaret, to run for his seat if he should die. She did and she won. In Congress, Representative Margaret Smith worked hard on military affairs, fighting to make sure Army and Navy nurses, mostly women, would receive benefits the way men did. In 1947, when a Maine Senate seat opened up, Margaret campaigned throughout the state and won 71% of the vote – the first woman to win a Senate seat in her own right. The Senate clearly did not welcome women – all the bathrooms were marked "men!"   But that didn't stop Margaret.

After World War II was over, the U.S. soon had a new enemy – the Soviet Union. Senator Joseph McCarthy began saying many people were Communists. People who had done nothing wrong lost their jobs and reputations. Other people were afraid to stand up to him for fear he might come after them. But on June 1st, 1950, Margaret Chase Smith bravely stood up in the Senate and made a "Declaration of Conscience" saying, *"The American people are sick and tired of being afraid to speak their minds lest they be politically smeared as 'Communists.'"* She accused him of *the "selfish political exploitation of fear, bigotry, ignorance, and intolerance."* Sadly, her speech didn't stop Senator McCarthy – he continued his "witch hunts" for another four years until the full Senate finally condemned his actions in 1954.

Ten years later, Senator Margaret Chase Smith again did something very surprising. She made a speech detailing the reasons why she shouldn't run for President of the United States, including the fact that no one thought she could win – then she said she was running anyway! She was the first woman to run for president from a major political party. She won votes in New Hampshire, Texas, Oregon, Massachusetts and Illinois but lost the Republican nomination to Barry Goldwater. In 1989, President George H.W. Bush awarded her the Presidential Medal of Freedom, the nation's highest civilian honor.

Fascinating Factoids: Margaret was a strong advocate for funding NASA's space program, saying that the investment would pay back tenfold in the knowledge gained. NASA's director, Dr. James Webb, went so far as to say, *"If it were not for...Senator Margaret Chase Smith, we never would have placed a man on the moon."*
Elizabeth Dole (1936-) ran as a Republican in the 2000 presidential election. In October 1999, she was in second place behind George W. Bush in the polls but couldn't get financing and pulled out before the primaries**.**

Read More – *for Kids:* **Madam President: The Extraordinary, True (and Evolving) Story of Women in Politics** by Catherine Thimmesh, 2004. **A woman in the House (and Senate)** by Ilene Cooper, 2014. *for Teens and Adults:* **No Place for a Woman: A Life of Senator Margaret Chase Smith** by Janann Sherman, 1999. **Politics of Conscience: A Biography of Margaret Chase Smith** by Patricia Ward Wallace, 1995. **Paving the Way for Madam President** by Nichola D. Gutgold, 2006.

Visit: Margaret Chase Smith Library Skowhegan, MA www.mcslibrary.org

*The first female senator who did not get her start as a politician's widow was **Nancy Kassebaum** (1932-) a moderate-to-liberal Republican who co-sponsored the Kennedy-Kassebaum Health Insurance Portability and Accountability Act. Nancy grew up in Kansas in a home full of politics – her father was the Republican Governor and had run as the Republican candidate for president in 1938. In the mid 1970s, she moved to Washington D.C. to work in the office of Kansas Republican Senator James Pearson. When he decided to retire in 1978, Nancy decided to run for his seat. Most people thought she'd never win – she had little experience and eight Republican primary challengers – but she had her family name and she pulled off the election. Nancy was a Republican from a conservative state but she often worked with Democrats including Senator Ted Kennedy on issues she believed in, including affordable health care and access to safe and legal abortion. She also worked hard as the head of the Foreign Relations Subcommittee on African Affairs to end South Africa's practice of apartheid (segregation by race). She stayed in the Senate for nearly 20 years – most of the time one of only one or two women there. She said she didn't think of herself as a woman senator but as a Senator from Kansas who happened to be a woman.

Margaret Chase Smith (1897-1995)

1st Female Senator Elected in her Own Right, 1st woman to Run for President from a Major Political Party

"If I am to be remembered in history, it will not be because of legislative accomplishments, but for an act I took as a legislator in the U.S. Senate when on June 1, 1950, I spoke...in condemnation of McCarthyism."

"When people keep telling you, you can't do a thing, you kind of like to try."
– Sen. Margaret Chase Smith announcing her candidacy for President of the United States in 1964."

Image by Laura Leigh Myers © 2016

FOR PRESIDENT
MARGARET CHASE SMITH

Lady Bird Johnson (1912-2007) Environmentalist and Activist First Lady

"Well, what did you do for women today" – Lady Bird's nightly query to her husband the President

When Claudia Alta Taylor was just a little girl, a family nurse declared, "She's as purty as a lady bird!" and the name stuck. Lady Bird grew up in a mansion in the bayou country of East Texas. Her father was a sharecropper's son who had become a rich cotton farmer and the owner of two general stores. When Lady Bird was five, her mother died. Her mother's sister moved in to take care of her, but Lady Bird spent much of her childhood alone outdoors among the tall pines and wildflowers – discovering a love for the environment she would retain all her life.

She graduated high school at age 15 and attended several colleges before eventually going to the University of Texas. Arriving in Austin by plane, Lady Bird was awed by the sight of a field covered with bluebonnets and instantly fell in love with the city. She majored in art and journalism and graduated with honors in 1934 with plans to become a reporter – but that year she met and married Lyndon Baines Johnson and ended up becoming involved in politics instead. She used part of her inheritance to finance his first run for Congress in 1937. Once in Washington D.C., she often helped her husband and even ran his congressional office after he enlisted in the Navy at the beginning of World War II. She also proved herself a savvy businesswoman – buying up radio and television stations (sometimes over her husband's objections), she turned an initial $41,000 investment into more than $150 million!

In 1960, John F. Kennedy chose Lyndon Johnson as his running mate and Lady Bird campaigned extensively for the ticket. On November 22, 1963, the Johnsons were two cars behind the Kennedys when the President was assassinated. All at once, under tragic circumstances, Lyndon Johnson became president – and Lady Bird Johnson became first lady. Knowing how flowers had helped with her own childhood grief, she created the First Lady's Committee for a More Beautiful Capital saying *"Where flowers bloom, so does hope."* She then expanded the idea to the whole country, lobbying congress to pass the Highway Beautification Act – the first major legislative campaign launched by a first lady. Nicknamed "Lady Bird's Bill," it aimed to remove signs and trash from national highways and plant wildflowers, bulbs, and trees along roadsides and call attention to the growing crisis of habitat and species loss.

Lady Bird transformed the office of the first lady. She was the first to have a press secretary and her own chief of staff, the first to have a liaison with Congress and the first to campaign extensively on her own for her husband. She held "Women Do-er Luncheons" where experts discussed issues and brainstormed solutions to the nation's social problems, and she advocated actively for legislation including Head Start and the 1964 Civil Rights Act. She was also the first to publish a book on her experiences as first lady, and she was an outspoken supporter of women's rights issues, calling the Equal Rights Amendment, *"the right thing to do."* Lady Bird remained an environmental activist all her life; at age 70, she co-founded (with actress Helen Hayes) the National Wildflower Research Center to collect and preserve seeds of wildflowers to protect them from extinction. When asked by reporters why she created the center, she told reporters it was her way of *"paying rent for the space I have taken up in this highly interesting world."*

Fascinating Factoid: Lady Bird was protected by the United States Secret Service for 44 years, longer than anyone else in history. She was honored with the country's highest civilian award, the Presidential Medal of Freedom in 1977, and was given the Congressional Gold Medal in 1988.

Read More – *for Kids:* **Miss Lady Bird's Wildflowers: How a First Lady Changed America** by Kathi Appelt, 2005. *for Teens and Adults:* **A White House diary** by Claudia Alta Johnson and Lady Bird Johnson, 1970. **Lady Bird Johnson: An Oral History** by Michael L. Gillette, 2012. **Lady Bird and Lyndon: The Hidden Story of a Marriage That Made a President** by Betty Boyd Caroli, 2015.

Visit: LBJ Library and Museum Austin, TX www.lbjlibrary.org
Lady Bird Johnson National Wildflower Research Center Austin, TX www.wildflower.org

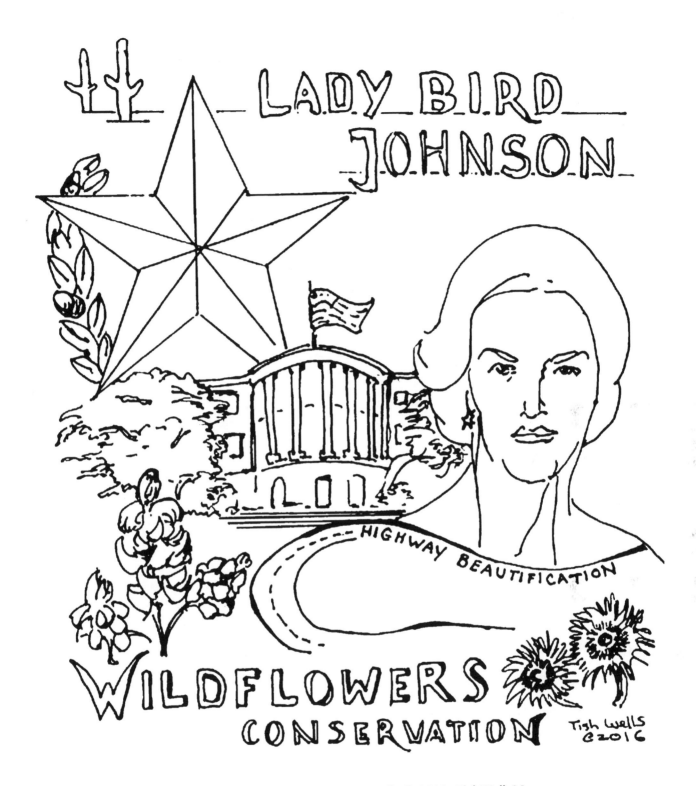

Lady Bird Johnson (1912-2007) by Tish Wells © 2016 TishWells14.com
Environmentalist and Activist First Lady – Chaired "Women Do-er Luncheons"

"The Constitution of the United States does not mention the First Lady. She is elected by one man only. The statute books assign her no duties and yet, when she gets the job, a podium is there if she cares to use it. I did."

Speaking before the American Institute of Architects in 1968:
*" The job really requires thoughtful interrelation of the whole environment. Not only in buildings, but parks, not only parks, but highways, not only highways, but open spaces and green belts....
beautification ...describes the whole effort to bring the natural world and the manmade world to harmony."*

Shirley Chisholm (1924-2005)
First Black Congresswoman and Presidential Candidate

"Unbought and Unbossed"

Born in Brooklyn to immigrant laborer parents, Shirley spent her primary school years with her grandmother in her parents' homeland of Barbados. She appreciated the excellent education she received there in a one room strict British-style school – writing in her 1970 autobiography, *"If I speak and write easily now, that early education is the main reason."* Shirley returned to the states in 1934 and later enrolled in the integrated Girl's High in Brooklyn, continuing on to get a B.A. at Brooklyn College. Though she was a prize debater there, she never dreamed of running for political office – *"Who would vote for a black woman with a Caribbean accent?"* She married, taught nursery school and earned a Masters in Education from the Teacher's College at Columbia University in 1952. Over the next decade, she became director of two day care centers.

Seeing the difficulties faced by the families she worked with, Shirley became an advocate for early education and child welfare. In 1965, she was elected to the New York State Assembly. There she succeeded in getting unemployment benefits extended to domestic workers and sponsored affirmative action legislation which gave disadvantaged students the chance to enter college. In 1968, when a new seat was created in a district with African American, Jewish, and Hispanic voters, Shirley decided to run and, after a tough race, she won. She was the nation's first black congresswoman. In Washington, she staffed her office entirely with women – surprising everyone since women in most Congressional offices were few and far between, with the exception of secretaries. She spoke out strongly against the Vietnam War calling it *"immoral, unjust, and unnecessary"* and said that the money spent on war would be much better spent helping people with housing, food, and educational programs.

In 1972, Shirley Chisholm decided to run for the highest office in the land – president! She knew she couldn't win but she wanted a way to speak to all of America about the poor, minorities, and the Vietnam War. She campaigned hard using the slogan *"Unbought and Unbossed"* and was fearless – she survived three assassination attempts – but won only 152 delegate votes at the Democratic convention, a tiny fraction of the 3000 needed to win. Shirley returned to Congress and continued to fight for the change she believed in. Later she became a professor at Mt. Holyoke College teaching politics and women's studies and co-founded the National Political Congress of Black Women. Once asked how she wished to be remembered, she said she'd like her gravestone to read *"Shirley Chisholm had guts."* In 2015, Shirley Chisholm was posthumously awarded the Presidential Medal of Freedom.

Fascinating Factoids: In the 2008 Democratic presidential primary season, Barack Obama and Hillary Rodham Clinton staged their historic 'firsts' battle – the victor would either be the first major party African American nominee, or the first woman nominee – but Chisholm's 1972 campaign paved the way for both of them!

America's first (and to date *only*) female African American Senator was **Carol Moseley Braun (1947-)** who represented Illinois from 1993 to 1999. She ran for the Democratic presidential nomination in 2003 but dropped out of the race after a disappointing finish in an early primary.

Read More – *for Kids:* **Shirley Chisholm** by Jill S. Pollack, 1994. *for Teens and Adults:* **Unbought and Unbossed** by Shirley Chisholm (Expanded 40th Anniversary Edition, 2010.) (Also 2005 DVD: *Chisholm '72: Unbought and Unbossed*), **Shirley Chisholm: Catalyst for Change**, by Barbara Winslow, 2014.

Visit: The Shirley Chisholm Center for Research on Women at Brooklyn College. Brooklyn, NY.
Smithsonian National Museum of African American History and Culture Washington DC nmaahc.si.edu

Shirley Chisholm (1924-2005) "Unbought and Unbossed" by Jill Obrig © 2016
First Black Congresswoman and Presidential Candidate

"When I die, I want to be remembered as a woman who lived in the twentieth century and who dared to be a catalyst for change. I don't want to be remembered as the first black woman who went to Congress, and I don't even want to be remembered as the first woman who happened to be black to make a bid for the presidency. I want to be remembered as a woman who fought for change in the twentieth century. That's what I want." – Shirley Chisholm

Rosalynn Carter (1927-)
"More a political partner than a political wife."

Rosalynn Carter was born in the farming community of Plains, Georgia, the eldest first of four children. When she was thirteen, her father died of cancer, and Rosalynn took a job at a beauty parlor to help her mother make ends meet. She graduated as valedictorian from high school and enrolled in a nearby community college. Money was tight – if she wanted to see a movie with friends, she skipped lunch. During this time, she met Jimmy Carter, her best friend's older brother, and a cadet at the Annapolis Naval Academy. When they were married in 1946, 19-year-old Rosalynn left college to move with her husband to Norfolk, Virginia, the first of several military moves. She continued her education in literature and art through home-study programs while raising four children. In 1953, following the death of Jimmy's father, they returned to Plains so Jimmy could run the family peanut business. Rosalynn took charge of the business's bookkeeping and then managed the entire business in her husband's absence when he was elected to the Georgia Senate in 1961. When Jimmy ran for governor of Georgia in 1970, Rosalynn campaigned for her husband and met constituents deeply affected by mental-health issues. After his election, she became their advocate – working to overhaul the state's mental-health system. In 1974, when Jimmy announced his candidacy for president, Rosalynn immediately began campaigning all around the country for her husband. She was the first candidate's wife to ever make a campaign promise of her own: that as first lady she would make the welfare of the nation's mentally ill her priority. In 1977, Jimmy Carter, with Rosalynn at his side, was sworn in as the 39th President of the United States.

Soon after the inauguration, Jimmy asked his wife to be his representative to establish good relations with leaders of a number of Latin American countries. Rosalynn brushed up her Spanish and had many briefings with State Department experts and Latin American scholars. In June 1977, Rosalynn, accompanied by State Department officials and Secret Service Agents, spent two weeks traveling around Latin America and the Caribbean, meeting with heads of state and sharing the results of the conversations with her husband by phone each night. The president was pleased with her work, but the press was critical since she was neither an elected official nor a professional diplomat. So, for the rest of his term, she limited herself to humanitarian missions.

Rosalynn continued her activism on mental health issues. She chaired the President's Commission on Mental Health. The resulting bill increased federal and state funding for the chronically mentally ill and created a bill of rights protecting the mentally ill from discrimination. Rosalynn testified about the bill before Congress and the Mental Health Systems Bill was passed in September of 1980. She did similar work for senior citizens, lobbying Congress for passage of the Age Discrimination Act, which lifted restrictions on the retirement age within the workforce. Rosalynn also presided over the White House Conference on Aging. After her husband left the presidency, Rosalynn continued to be a leading advocate for mental health, caregivers, early childhood immunization, human rights, and conflict resolution. She also worked to address the unmet needs of U.S. soldiers returning from Iraq and Afghanistan. She has won many honors including the Presidential Medal of Freedom, America's highest civilian honor.

Fascinating Factoid: Rosalynn Carter considered herself *"more a political partner than a political wife."* And she was. She visited 18 foreign countries and 27 American cities, attended 259 private meetings and 50 public meetings, delivered 15 major speeches, gave 32 interviews and 22 press conferences, and hosted 83 official receptions. She had a business lunch meeting with her husband, President Jimmy Carter each week and in 1980, became the first First Lady to attend presidential cabinet meetings.

Read More – *for Kids:* **Rosalynn Carter: Steel Magnolia** by Ruth Turk, 1997. **Mrs. Carter's Butterfly Garden** by Steve Rich, 2014. *for Teens and Adults:* **Rosalynn Carter: Equal Partner in the White House** by Scott Kaufman, 2007. **First Lady from Plains** by Rosalynn Carter, 1984.

Visit: The Jimmy Carter Library and Museum. Atlanta, Georgia. www.jimmycarterlibrary.gov

Rosalynn Carter (1927-) by Holly Bess Kincaid © 2016

"I am the person closest to the President of the United States, and if I can explain his policies and let the people of Latin America know of his great interest and friendship, I intend to do so."

*"A leader takes people where they want to go.
A great leader takes people where they don't necessarily want to go, but ought to be."*

Geraldine Ferraro (1935-2011)
First Female Vice Presidential Candidate of a Major American Political Party

Geraldine was born in 1935 in a small town in New York State. Though it was the middle of the Great Depression, her family was reasonably comfortable since her Italian immigrant father owned two restaurants. However, when she was eight, her father died from a heart attack. The family had to move to a low-income area in the South Bronx and her mother got a job as a seamstress in a clothing factory. Despite their economic struggles, Geraldine's mother was adamant that her daughter get a good education, and Geraldine was able to go to a Catholic boarding school. Geraldine was an excellent student and was voted "most likely to succeed" when she graduated in 1952. Her uncle's attitude was more typical: *"Why bother? She's pretty. She's a girl. She'll get married."* Geraldine enrolled in college with money from a scholarship and multiple jobs. She received a Bachelor of Arts in English in 1956, the first woman in her family to earn a college degree. After graduation, she got a job as an elementary school teacher *"because that's what women were supposed to do"* but soon decided she wanted to be a lawyer. An admissions officer at the law school remarked *"I hope you're serious, Gerry. You're taking a man's place, you know."* Geraldine went to classes at night while teaching second grade during the day and still managed to graduate with honors from Fordham Law School – one of only two women in her graduating class. After she passed her bar exam in 1960, she married, had children and worked as a private-practice lawyer. In 1974, Geraldine became an assistant district attorney in Queens New York and helped set up a bureau to help women who had been the victims of violence or abuse. When she found out that she wasn't getting the same pay as her male co-workers, she decided to run for Congress to change the laws.

Geraldine was elected to the House in 1978 from a conservative district in Queens, NY on the slogan *"Finally, a tough Democrat."* Once in Congress, she worked hard on legislation to bring equality for women in the areas of wages, pensions, and retirement plans as well as other issues affecting women, children, and the elderly. Democratic politicians liked this tough, straight-talking woman and, in 1984, they decided she'd make a good Vice Presidential Candidate alongside Walter Mondale. They chose her over Congresswoman Pat Schroeder, in part because they thought she'd appeal both to women and Italian Americans. When she accepted the nomination, the crowd at the Democratic National Convention went wild. Thousands of letters poured in every day. Girls wanted to vote even though they were too young. Women who had never before voted asked how. Some women sent campaign contributions in secret – fearing their husbands wouldn't approve! Despite an excellent performance in the Vice Presidential debate and a good rapport with voters, Geraldine's lack of foreign policy experience and concerns about her husband's business practices hurt the campaign. The Democrats lost the election in a landslide to Ronald Reagan and George Bush. In her concession speech, she remarked *"The race is over. My candidacy has said the days of discrimination are numbered. American women will never be second-class citizens again."*

Geraldine ran for Senate in 1992 and 1998 but lost both campaigns. She served as President Bill Clinton's United States Ambassador to the United Nations Commission on Human Rights from 1993 until 1996. She also worked as a journalist, author, cancer activist, businesswoman, and advisor in the 2008 presidential campaign of Senator Hillary Clinton.

Fascinating Factoids: Belva Lockwood's running mate in 1884 was female. The Republican Party would nominate their first woman Vice Presidential candidate in the election of 2008 when Sarah Palin joined the ticket with John McCain.

Read More – *for Kids:* **Madam President: The Extraordinary, True (and Evolving) Story of Women in Politics** by Catherine Thimmesh, 2008. *for Teens and Adults:* **Ferraro: My Story** by Geraldine Ferraro, 1985. **Changing History: Women, Power and Politics** by Geraldine A. Ferraro, 1993. **Paving the Way for Madam President** by Nichola D. Gutgold and Geraldine Ferraro, 2006. **Video: Geraldine Ferraro: Paving the Way**, 2014.

Geraldine Ferraro (1935-2011) by Tish Wells © 2016 TishWells14.com

" I stand before you to proclaim tonight America is the land where dreams can come true for all of us.
If we can do this, we can do anything."
— Geraldine Ferraro's acceptance speech for the 1984 Vice Presidential nomination.

Hillary Rodham Clinton (1947-)
First Woman Nominee for President from a Major American Political Party

*"I'm often asked if what I am doing in Washington creates a new role model for first ladies...
and I always say I don't want to create any new stereotype...I want all women to be given
the respect they deserve to have for the choices they may make."*

As a girl, Hillary wanted to be an astronaut – but when she wrote a letter to NASA asking how, they wrote back that there was no such thing as a woman astronaut. There were no girls allowed. So instead of going to the moon, Hillary decided she would change things on her own planet. Though she encountered significant discrimination against women along the way, Hillary became a lawyer. After graduation from Yale Law School in 1973, she worked at the Children's Defense Fund. Then after marrying fellow lawyer Bill Clinton, she became a law professor, the first female partner at the largest law firm in Arkansas and Arkansas's First Lady after her husband won the Governor's race.

When Bill Clinton was elected President in 1992, Hillary Rodham Clinton was the first First Lady to get an office in the West Wing – the "power center" of the White House – previous presidential wives had been relegated to the East Wing. Following Rosalynn Carter's example, she traveled all over the world as her husband's representative – advocating for equal rights for women and children, tolerance, and democratic reforms. Her husband also appointed her to chair the Presidential Task Force on National Health Care Reform. However, significant Republican opposition and a national negative advertising campaign thwarted her efforts to get a national health care program in place.

After her husband's presidency ended in 2000, Hillary traded her unofficial role in government for an official one. She ran for the U.S Senate – and won – becoming U.S. Senator from New York and the first First Lady to hold elected office. In 2008, she ran for President but lost the nomination to Barack Obama. He appointed her Secretary of State, a role she held for 4 years – negotiating with governments and continuing to speak out on behalf of women and children – globetrotting 957,744 miles (four times the distance to the moon!) and visiting 112 countries – a record. She was the third female Secretary of State and the first former First Lady to hold a cabinet office.

In 2016, she accomplished another first – becoming the first woman to become a major party's nominee for President. But Hillary Rodham Clinton did not become president. In an upset almost no one predicted, she lost the election to Republican Donald Trump.. Even though she won the popular vote, she lost the electoral college.

Read More *(a sampling)* **for Kids: Hillary** by Jonah Winter, 2016. **Hillary Rodham Clinton: Dreams Taking Flight** by Kathleen Krull, 2016. **Who is Hillary Clinton?** by Heather Alexander, 2016. *for Teens and Adults:* **Hillary Clinton: American Woman of the World** by Cheryl Harness, 2016. **A Woman in Charge** by Carl Bernstein, 2007. **Stronger Together**, 2016. **Hard Choices**, 2015. **Living History**, 2003 – all by Hillary Rodham Clinton.

Fascinating Factoid: Hillary's mother, Dorothy, was born on June 4, 1919 – the very day that the 19th Amendment giving women the right to vote was finally passed by Congress! When Dorothy was a young child, she was often left alone, cold and hungry in her family's Chicago apartment. At age eight, she was sent to live with her grandparents in California and then, when she was fourteen, Dorothy's grandparents threw her out of the house – telling her she was old enough to support herself. Luckily she found a job as a maid with a family who allowed her to continue going to school but throughout her teenage years, she constantly worried that she would be homeless and hungry. Hillary's daughter, Chelsea, tells this story and shows young people how they can help the world's less privileged in her book **It's Your World: Get Informed, Get Inspired and Get Going!** (2015).

Visit: Clinton House Museum, Fayetteville, AR. www.clintonhousemuseum.org
William J. Clinton Presidential Library and Museum, Little Rock AR.   www.clintonlibrary.gov
The White House, Washington DC   www.nps.gov/whho

Hillary Rodham Clinton (1947-) by Jill Schmidt © 2016

*"'This loss hurts. But please, please never stop believing that fighting for what's right is worth it.
It's always worth it. And we need you keep up these fights now and for the rest of your lives."
– from her Presidential concession speech on November 9, 2016*

"Take a risk, and dare to change the world."

"STRONGER TOGETHER"
Excerpts from Michelle Obama's Speech at the 2016 Democratic Convention

"...With every word we utter, with every action we take, we know our kids are watching us... our words and actions matter, not just to our girls, but the children across this country... every election is about who will have the power to shape our children for the next four or eight years of their lives...

I trust Hillary to lead this country because I've seen her lifelong devotion to our nation's children, not just her own daughter, who she has raised to perfection...but every child who needs a champion, kids who take the long way to school to avoid the gangs, kids who wonder how they'll ever afford college, kids whose parents don't speak a word of English, but dream of a better life, kids who look to us to determine who and what they can be...Hillary has spent decades doing the relentless, thankless work to actually make a difference in their lives...advocating for kids with disabilities as a young lawyer, fighting for children's health care as first lady, and for quality child care in the Senate.

And when she didn't win the nomination eight years ago, she didn't get angry or disillusioned...she proudly stepped up to serve our country once again as secretary of state, traveling the globe to keep our kids safe... there were plenty of moments when Hillary could have decided that this work was too hard, that the price of public service was too high, that she was tired of being picked apart for how she looks or how she talks or even how she laughs. But here's the thing. What I admire most about Hillary is that she never buckles under pressure. She never takes the easy way out. And Hillary Clinton has never quit on anything in her life.

And when I think about the kind of president that I want for my girls and all our children, that's what I want. I want someone with the proven strength to persevere, someone who knows this job and takes it seriously, someone who understands that the issues a president faces are not black and white and cannot be boiled down to 140 characters. Because when you have the nuclear codes at your fingertips and the military in your command, you can't make snap decisions. You can't have a thin skin or a tendency to lash out. You need to be steady and measured and well-informed.

I want a president with a record of public service, someone whose life's work shows our children that we don't chase fame and fortune for ourselves, we fight to give everyone a chance to succeed. And we give back even when we're struggling ourselves because we know that there is always someone worse off. And there but for the grace of God go I. I want a president who will teach our children that everyone in this country matters, a president who truly believes in the vision that our Founders put forth all those years ago that we are all created equal, each a beloved part of the great American story.

And when crisis hits, we don't turn against each other. No, we listen to each other, we lean on each other, because we are always stronger together....You see, Hillary understands that the president is about one thing and one thing only, it's about leaving something better for our kids. That's how we've always moved this country forward, by all of us coming together on behalf of our children... because they know it takes a village...

Hillary Clinton .. has the guts and the grace to keep coming back and putting those cracks in that highest and hardest glass ceiling until she finally breaks through, lifting all of us along with her.

That is the story of this country... the story of generations of people who felt the lash of bondage, the shame of servitude, the sting of segregation, but who kept on striving and hoping and doing ...so that today I wake up every morning in a house that was built by slaves. And I watch my daughters, two beautiful, intelligent, black young women playing with their dogs on the White House lawn.

And because of Hillary Clinton, my daughters and all our sons and daughters now take for granted that a woman can be president of the United States..." – Michelle Obama, July 2016

Ms. magazine cover rendered by Victoria Ford - Reprinted by permission of *Ms.* magazine, © 2012

But Hillary Rodham Clinton did not become president. Though she won the popular vote, she lost the Electoral College – here are excerpts of her speech to her supporters:

"Last night, I congratulated Donald Trump and offered to work with him on behalf of our country. I hope that he will be a successful president for all Americans.

This is not the outcome we wanted or we worked so hard for, and I'm sorry we did not win this election for the values we share and the vision we hold for our country. But I feel pride and gratitude for this wonderful campaign that we built together –- this vast, diverse, creative, unruly, energized campaign. You represent the best of America, and being your candidate has been one of the greatest honors of my life.

I know how disappointed you feel, because I feel it too. And so do tens of millions of Americans who invested their hopes and dreams in this effort. This is painful, and it will be for a long time. But I want you to remember this: Our campaign was never about one person or even one election. It was about the country we love – and about building an America that's hopeful, inclusive, and big-hearted.

We have seen that our nation is more deeply divided than we thought. But I still believe in America — and I always will. And if you do, too, then we must accept this result –- and then look to the future. Donald Trump is going to be our president. We owe him an open mind and the chance to lead. Our constitutional democracy enshrines the peaceful transfer of power, and we don't just respect that, we cherish it. It also enshrines other things — the rule of law, the principle that we're all equal in rights and dignity, and the freedom of worship and expression. We respect and cherish these things too – and we must defend them.

And let me add: Our constitutional democracy demands our participation, not just every four years, but all the time. So let's do all we can to keep advancing the causes and values we all hold dear: making our economy work for everyone, not just those at the top; protecting our country and protecting our planet; and breaking down all the barriers that hold anyone back from achieving their dreams.

We've spent a year and a half bringing together millions of people from every corner of our country to say with one voice that we believe that the American Dream is big enough for everyone – for people of all races and religions, for men and women, for immigrants, for LGBT people, and people with disabilities. Our responsibility as citizens is to keep doing our part to build that better, stronger, fairer America we seek. And I know you will.

I am so grateful to stand with all of you. ..I will always be grateful to the creative, talented, dedicated men and women at our headquarters in Brooklyn and across our country who poured their hearts into this campaign. For you veterans, this was a campaign after a campaign – for some of you, this was your first campaign ever. I want each of you to know that you were the best campaign anyone has had. To all the volunteers, community leaders, activists, and union organizers who knocked on doors, talked to neighbors, posted on Facebook - even in secret or in private: Thank you. To everyone who sent in contributions as small as $5 and kept us going, thank you.

And to all the young people in particular, I want you to hear this. I've spent my entire adult life fighting for what I believe in. I've had successes and I've had setbacks –- sometimes really painful ones. Many of you are at the beginning of your careers. You will have successes and setbacks, too. This loss hurts. But please, please never stop believing that fighting for what's right is worth it. It's always worth it. And we need you keep up these fights now and for the rest of your lives. To all the women, and especially the young women, who put their faith in this campaign and in me, I want you to know that nothing has made me prouder than to be your champion.

I know that we still have not shattered that highest glass ceiling. But some day someone will — hopefully sooner than we might think right now... And to all of the little girls watching this, never doubt that you are valuable and powerful and deserving of every chance and opportunity in the world to pursue and achieve your own dreams... "

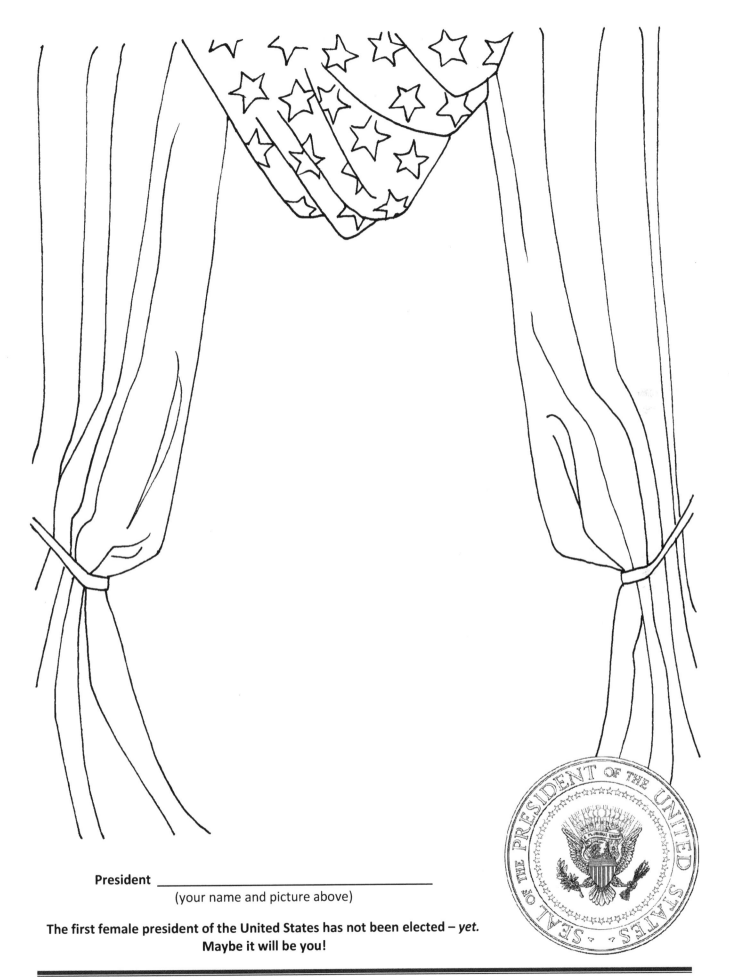

President _____

(your name and picture above)

The first female president of the United States has not been elected – *yet*.
Maybe it will be you!

Some of the Women Who Have Run for President

1872: Victoria Claflin Woodhull of the Equal Rights Party, the first woman to run for the highest office (ran again in 1892)

1884 and 1888: Belva Ann Lockwood ran for president on the Equal Right's Party ticket in 1884 and 1888 (her running mate, Marietta Stow, was also female)

1940: Gracie Allen with her husband George Burns, traveled around the country on a farcical run for the presidency for the "Surprise Party" under the slogan *"Down with Common Sense - Vote for Gracie Allen"*

1960: Whitney Slocomb (Greenback Party)

1964: Margaret Chase Smith, a Republican, first woman to seek the nomination of a major political party and the first woman to be placed in nomination at a major party convention

1968: Charlene Mitchell (Communist Party USA)

1972: Shirley Chisholm (Democrat - first African American candidate from a major party), **Patsy Mink** (Democrat - first Asian American woman to run for president), **Linda Jenness** (Socialist Workers Party), **Evelyn Reed** (Socialist Workers Party)

1976: Margaret Wright (Peace and Freedom Party – Dr. Benjamin Spock was her running mate) and **Ellen McCormack** (ran again in 1980)

1980: Deirdre Griswold and **Maureen Smith** (Peace and Freedom Party)

1984: Sonia Johnson (U.S. Citizens Party) and **Isabelle Masters** (who also ran in 1992 and 1996 and 2000 and 2004 in the self-founded "Looking Back Party")

1988: Patricia Schroeder (Democrat) and **Willa Kenoyer** and **Lenora Fulani** (New Alliance Party – again in 1992)

1992: Gloria La Riva (Workers World Party) and **Helen Halyard** (Socialist Equality Party)

1996: Marsha Feinland and **Mary Hollis** and **Diane Templin** and **Elvana Lloyd-Duffie** and **Monica Moorehead** (ran again in 2000)

2000: Elizabeth Dole (Republican) and **Cathy Brown**

2004: Carol Moseley Braun (Democrat)

2008 Hillary Rodham Clinton (Democrat) and **Cynthia McKinney** (Green Party)

2012: Rosanne Barr (Peace and Freedom Party) **and Jill Stein** (Green Party, ran again in 2016)

2016: Carly Fiorina (Republican) and **Hillary Rodham Clinton** (Democrat, first woman nominee for president from a major party)

A complete list can be found at: en.wikipedia.org/wiki/List_of_female_United_States_presidential_and_vice-presidential_candidates

A Short History of Women's Suffrage in the U.S.

1648 Margaret Brent becomes the first American woman to demand the right to vote. She actually demands two votes in the colony of Maryland's assembly —one for herself as one of the largest landowners in the colony and one on behalf of the deceased Lord Baltimore, whose estate she was managing. She is turned down.

1792 Mary Wollstonecraft's *The Vindication of the Rights of Women* **is published in London.** She argues that allowing women to vote would be good for society since women are the spiritual equals of men and, if given a proper education, could be man's intellectual equal. Her writings inspire Elizabeth Cady Stanton and Susan B. Anthony.

1787 - U.S. Constitutional Convention gives states the right to decide on voting qualifications – and only New Jersey gives women the right to vote (a 1776 New Jersey law gave the vote to all adults with property over a certain value. Married women couldn't vote because the husband technically owned the property but single women and widows could – indeed a 1790 New Jersey law even referred to voters as "he or she." But when a large number of women voted in the 1800 presidential election, the legislature decided to change the law and in 1807, voting was confined to white men.)

1807 – New Jersey revokes women's right to vote.

July 19-30, 1848 – Elizabeth Cady Stanton, Lucretia Mott, and three other women organize the first U.S. women's rights convention in Seneca Falls, New York. Three hundred people attend and 68 women and 32 men sign the "Declaration of Sentiments" which outlines the wrongs done to women and demands that all female citizens be given the right to vote.

1850 – Lucy Stone and Paulina Kellogg Wright Davis organize the first National Women's Rights Convention in Worcester, Massachusetts.

1851 Sojourner Truth delivers her famous "Ain't I a Woman?" speech.

1866 – Elizabeth Cady Stanton and Susan B. Anthony create the American Equal Rights Association (AERA). Their goal is suffrage for women and African-Americans. Susan B. Anthony presents Congress with petitions signed by thousands of Americans asking for the vote for women.

1868 – 14th Amendment ratified – all "citizens" (defined as male) granted equal protection of the Constitution.

1869 – Wyoming Territory grants women the right to vote – 1st American female suffrage since New Jersey lost it in 1807.

1869 – 15th Amendment gives African American men the right to vote.

1869 – Women's suffrage movement splits into two groups:
May 1869 – **National Woman Suffrage Association (NWSA)** formed with Elizabeth Cady Stanton as president opposes the 15th Amendment unless it gave votes to women.
November 1869 – **American Woman Suffrage Association (AWSA)** formed with Henry Ward Beecher as president sees the 15th Amendment as a stepping stone to women's suffrage and supports a state-by-state strategy for achieving women's suffrage.

1870 – Utah Territory grants women the right to vote – revoked in 1887.

1872 – Victoria Woodhull nominated for president by the Equal Rights Party. She suspends her campaign before Election Day and does not receive any official votes.

November 5, 1872 – Susan B. Anthony attempts to vote for Grant in the presidential election. She is arrested and brought to trial in Rochester, New York in June 1873. **Sojourner Truth tries to vote in Battle Creek, Michigan but is refused a ballot.**

Jan. 10, 1873 – The "Anthony Amendment" (named for Susan B. Anthony) for women's suffrage is introduced in Congress but fails.

Feb. 15, 1879 – Belva Ann Lockwood 's bill (H.R. 1077) allowing women to argue cases before the Supreme Court is signed into law by President Hayes.

1880 The Women's Christian Temperance Union under the leadership of Frances Willard decides to support women's suffrage.

1884 – Belva Ann Lockwood runs for President as the candidate from the Equal Rights Party. She and her female Vice President get over 4000 votes. She runs again in 1884 but receives few votes.

1890 – The two main women's suffrage organizations reunite to become the National American Woman Suffrage Association (NAWSA), led by Elizabeth Cady Stanton and Susan B. Anthony.

1896 – Idaho grants women suffrage.
1907 – Harriot Stanton Blatch organizes the Equality League of Self-Supporting Women. She attracts factory workers and other working women to the suffrage movement.

1910 – Washington State grants women suffrage.
1911 – California grants women suffrage.

1912 – The Progressive (Republican) Party headed by Theodore Roosevelt adopts women's suffrage as a plank in its platform – the first major party to do so.

1912 - Oregon, Arizona, and Kansas grant women suffrage.
1913 – Alaska Territory grants women suffrage.

March 3, 1913 – Organized by Alice Paul, 5000-8000 women march down Pennsylvania Avenue in Washington DC demanding the right to vote. The parade is led by suffragette Inez Milholland astride a white horse.

1915 – Carrie Chapman Catt becomes president of the National American Woman Suffrage Association and creates her "Winning Plan" – jointly working toward state-by-state suffrage and a Constitutional amendment.

Nov. 7, 1916 – Jeannette Rankin from Montana becomes the first female member of Congress.

1917 – North Dakota, Indiana, Nebraska, Michigan, and Arkansas grant limited suffrage to women; New York, South Dakota, and Oklahoma grant women the right to vote in all elections.

Alice Paul and the National Women's Party adopt more active methods to publicize the movement, including picketing the White House year-round. Arrested, jailed, and force-fed, they attract national attention and sympathy for the movement and eventually Woodrow Wilson's advocacy for the amendment in Congress.

June 4, 1919 – Congress approves the 19th Amendment to the Constitution.

Aug. 26, 1920 – 19th Amendment with identical wording to the 1878 "Anthony Amendment" is ratified by the 36th state –Tennessee – and (white) women across the country finally have the right to vote. (Women of Color have to wait longer: Native Americans aren't considered citizens and can't vote until 1924; Chinese-Americans are denied suffrage until 1943; Japanese-Americans until 1952; and Southern States soon enact literacy tests and other barriers effectively preventing many African-Americans from voting until the 1965 Voting Rights Act.)

1923 – The Equal Rights Amendment (ERA) proposed by Alice Paul is sent to Congress. *"Equality of rights under the law shall not be denied or abridged by the United States or by any state on account of sex."* Forty nine years later, Congress finally passes the proposed 27th Amendment on March 22, 1972 with a seven year deadline for ratification, but opposition forms and only 35 of the 38 needed states ratify the amendment in time. **To date, the ERA is still not the law of the land.**

Further Reading:

America's Daughters: 400 Years of American Women by Judith Head. Perspective, 1999.

A is for Abigail: An Almanac of Amazing American Women by Lynne Cheney and Robin Preiss Glasser. Simon and Schuster, 2003. (has timeline under U.S.)

Famous American Women (Dover History Coloring Book) by Gregory Guiteras. Dover, 2001.

Fight Like a Girl: 50 Feminists Who Changed the World by Laura Barcella. Zest Books, 2016.

Founding Mothers: Remembering the Ladies by Cokie Roberts. HarperCollins, 2014.

Founding Mothers: The Women Who Raised Our Nation by Cokie Roberts. Harper, 2005.

Independent Dames by Laurie Halse Anderson. Simon and Schuster, 2008.

Ladies of Liberty: the Women Who Shaped our Nation by Cokie Roberts. William Morrow, 2008.

Herstory: Women Who Changed the World edited by Ruth Ashby and Deborah Gore Ohrn. Viking, 1995.

The Highest Glass Ceiling: Women's Quest for the Presidency by Ellen Fitzpatrick. Harvard University Press, 2016.

Ladies First: 40 Daring American Women Who Were Second to None by Elizabeth Cody Kimmel. National Geographic, 2005.

Madam President: the Extraordinary, True (and Evolving) Story of Women in Politics by Catherine Thimmesh. Houghton Mifflin, 2004.

Mary Lincoln's Flannel Pajamas by Feather Schwartz Foster. Koehlerbooks, 2016.

The New York Public Library Amazing Women in American History: a Book of Answers for Kids by Sue Heinemann. John Wiley, 1998.

Rabble Rousers: 20 Women Who Made a Difference by Cheryl Harness. Dutton, 2003.

Rad American Women A-Z: Rebels, Trailblazers, and Visionaries who Shaped Our History . . . and Our Future! by Kate Schatz and Miriam Klein Stahl. City Lights/Sister Spit, 2015.

Remember the Ladies : 100 Great American Women by Cheryl Harness. HarperCollins, 2001.

Rightfully Ours: How Women Won the Vote in 21 Activities by Kerrie Logan Hollihan, 2012.

Scholastic Encyclopedia of Women in the United States by Sheila Keenan. Scholastic, 1996.

She Takes a Stand: 16 Fearless Activists Who Have Changed the World by Michael Elsohn Ross, Chicago Review Press, 2015.

Sisters in Strength: American Women Who Made a Difference by Yona Zeldis McDonough. Henry Holt, 2000.

Why Couldn't Susan B. Anthony Vote? And Other Questions About Women's Suffrage by Mary Kay Carson. Sterling, 2015.

With Courage and Cloth: Winning the Fight for a Woman's Right to Vote by Ann Bausem. Natl Geographic, 2004.

A Woman in the House (and Senate): How Women Came to the United States Congress, Broke Down Barriers, and Changed the Country by Ilene Cooper and Elizabeth Baddeley. Abrams, 2014.

Women Who Changed the World: 50 Amazing Americans by Laurie Calkhoven and Patricia Castelao, 2015.

You Wouldn't Want to Be a Suffragist! by Fiona Macdonald, 2009.

Our Illustrators:

Aarti Arora (Ella Baker, Elouise Pepion Cobell)
Aarti Arora is a professional graphic and textile designer with more than ten years of experience. She has created the company "Designer Connection" and is currently working as freelancer for various clients. She lives in New Jersey with her husband and two kids. Contact her at: aartiraj@gmail.com

Aileen Wu (Sonia Sotomayor)
Aileen Wu is a Princeton based digital illustrator. She's received various Scholastic Art and Writing awards and has been published in Alexandria Quarterly. She also illustrates for her school newspaper and local organizations. Contact her at: xx.aileen.wu@gmail.com

Aditi Tandon (Elizabeth Warren)
Aditi Tandon is a designer and an entrepreneur with over 17 years of business experience with Two Dotts (www.twodotts.com) her design company which offers specialized Graphic and UX Design Consulting services and an Etsy store which serves as an outlet for her gifts and patented product designs. She is also co-founder of Maroon Oak (www.maroonoak.com) a free networking and skill sharing community for all career women. Contact her at: aditi@MaroonOak.com

Amber McGonegal (Harriot Stanton Blatch)
Amber McGonegal is a student artist from central Jersey planning to study either illustration or digital media. She loves dogs, comics, and animation! Contact her at: amberdawn912@yahoo.com

Arlene Holmes (Elizabeth Gurley Flynn, Esther Morris, Anna Howard Shaw, Francis Perkins, Victoria Woodhull, Belva Lockwood, Eleanor Roosevelt)
Arlene Holmes is an artist and elementary school art teacher who works in different mediums such as oil, pastel, watercolor and colored pencils. She has worked with students for twenty five years and taught adult classes as well. Favorite subjects are landscapes and still lifes. She lives and works in the Hudson Valley of New York. Contact her at: avholmes@hvc.rr.com

B a r b a r a Schneider (Lucy Stone, Lucretia Mott)
B a r b a r a Schneider is a multiple-media / textile artist and designer. She has a great passion for toys and children´s literature, fashion and photography. Some themes are re-design, childhood and the discussion of humanity, our modern life and "our world cultures." She has participated in international juried group art and design exhibitions, projects and contests and received international awards and recognitions. Works of art have been published in international design and art books. Website: B a r b a r a Schneider @artavita.com

Caroline Mack (Mary Katherine Goddard)
Caroline Mack is a San Diego born set designer and decorator who is currently working in Los Angeles. She is a recent graduate of the UCLA School of Theater Film and Television. Website: www.carolinemackdesign.com

Caroline Yorke (Wilma Mankiller)
Caroline Yorke is a woman's history lover as well as an up and coming visual and performing artist based in New Jersey. Contact her at carolineyorke.com

Crina Magalio (Abigail Adams)
Crina is currently studying as a junior illustration major at Maryland Institute College of Art. She was born in Romania and was adopted by her loving parents in 1997. She has created a musical-themed mural and drawn illustrations for a children's book, and loves comic cons as a Disney, Star Wars, and Doctor Who geek. She also doodles dog characters and creates button designs for clients. Website: crinamagalioillustration.blogspot.com

Diana Wilkoc Patton (Phillis Wheatley, Sacajawea)
Diana is a watercolorist who has won over 135 awards, and has been teaching watercolor for over thirty years. Diana is a member of the American Artists Professional League, the Garden State Watercolor Society, and the NJ

Water Color Society. As an illustrator/author, Diana has two picture books, **Charlemagne to the Rescue** and **Rocking out to Sea.** **Ronnie's Friend Trike** is due out December 2016. She is a member of the Society of Children's Book Writers and Illustrators. Websites:www.dianapatton.com and www.charlemagnethefish.com

Holly Bess Kincaid (Rosalynn Carter)
Holly Bess Kincaid is the resident "Art Lady" at Skyline Middle School in Harrisonburg, Virginia. She refers to her classroom as the "Capitol of Creativity" and strives to create a studio environment where her students gain artistic skills and knowledge to help them express themselves through their visual voice. Holly Bess can be reached on Twitter and Instagram: @ArtLadyHBK Or her educational website: capitolofcreativity.weebly.com

Jasmine Florentine (Harriet Tubman)
Jasmine Florentine is a mechanical engineer and an artist from Los Angeles. After studying in Boston and traveling abroad for a few years, she now lives in New Hampshire. She works for FIRST robotics, playing with servos, gears, and powertools, and trying to inspire children like you to become the engineers and Historical Figures of Tomorrow. Website: jasmineflorentine.com

Jen Wistuba (Edith Bolling Wilson)
Jen Wistuba is a central NJ born artist and art educator, specializing in customized fine art portraits, including her unique Word Play Portraits, which she is often commissioned to do for weddings and anniversaries. Jen looks to expand her business by teaching Paint/Craft Parties as well as private art lessons. Currently working in the public school system, she strives to find unique ways to make cross-curricular connections, allowing art to be the bridge to higher learning. Email her at: JenWistuba@aol.com

Jill Obrig (Sojourner Truth, Ruth Bader Ginsburg, Shirley Chisholm)
Jill Obrig has been creating and teaching art for over 30 years and received a New York State Arts Mid-Hudson Grant in 2016 bridging children's literature with art history and art projects. She teaches painting in her Stone Ridge Studio to students from 6-89 years of age and shows her photography and art in various galleries throughout the Hudson Valley. She also teaches art at various museums including Partners at Olana State Museum and the Parrish Art Museum in Southampton, NY. To reach her for art education or show her work, email her at: jill.obrig@gmail.com

Jill Schmidt (Margaret Sanger, Gloria Steinem, Hillary Rodham Clinton)
Jill Schmidt has worked in commercial design and illustration, both in large advertising houses and as a freelance artist, since 1970. Her wide range of work includes illustrations for several children's books, designs for more than 75 book covers for Puzzazz Inc, mobile app interfaces, decorated accessories, and custom body art for Burning Man. She is the creative co-founder and art director of an interactive media startup, Minerva Interactive.

Jody Flegal (Juliette Gordon Low)
Jody Flegal's artistic interests and endeavors span many years. During her early twenties she was successful creating floral designs on velvet with oils and she exhibited and sold her paintings at several art shops. She has also experimented with faux finishes, murals, and decorative furniture and exploring different mediums such as watercolor, pastel, oil, and graphite. Her present interest is landscape and still life painting.

Judy Hnat (Septima Poinsette Clark)
Judy Hnat studied architecture at the University of Virginia and has been working in illustration and fine art ever since. She is delighted to have found such a rich and vibrant arts community near her home in Hunterdon County, NJ, where she has continued her studies at the Hunterdon Art Museum, the Center for Contemporary Art, and the Visual Arts Center of New Jersey. Her work has been exhibited at the Paper Mill Playhouse in Millburn, and the ACME Screening Room in Lambertville. While working in a wide variety of mediums she is most inspired when expressing the miracles she finds in nature. Webpage: facebook.com/judyhnat.art

Julie Goetz (Zitkala-Ša)
Julie Goetz is an artist living in Bedminster NJ. She finds inspiration for her painting from her animals and nature.

Justine Turnbull (Bella Abzug)
Justine Turnbull is a software engineer, designer, foodie, and amateur botanist based in San Francisco. Follow her work on Instagram @succsinthecity

Kat Schroeder (Sarah and Angelina Grimke)
Kat Schroeder is a San Diego based artist who has been involved in the arts since the age of 4. She has studied art at multiple academies including US Arts and UCSD as well as with a variety of local working artists. Kat's art has been exhibited in both local cafes and the San Diego County Fair where she has won three Best of Show ribbons. For the past 3 years, she has been teaching drawing and painting to young students. Kat is currently a sophomore in college earning her degrees in both Studio Arts and Psychology.

Kim Huyler Defibaugh (Dolley Madison)
Kim Huyler Defibaugh worked for Toms River Regional Schools (NJ) for 36 years, many years as an elementary art on a cart teacher and 11 years as Supervisor of Fine Arts. Primarily a fiber artist with an interest in repurposing materials, Kim's art has been exhibited in galleries and museums in New Jersey and Virginia. Recently she has produced illustrations for children's books. Kim has taken on state, regional and national leadership roles in art education organizations. She is Past-President of the Art Educators of NJ and Art Administrators of NJ, former Vice-President of the Eastern Region of the National Art Education Association, and is currently on the Board of Trustees for the National Art Education Foundation. Contact her at: drkimbeg@cox.net

Kim Wood (Frances Ellen Watkins Harper, Fanny Lou Hamer, Patricia Schroeder, Nancy Pelosi)
Kim Wood is a NJ based children's market illustrator and designer as well as a coloring book enthusiast. She is excited to have been able to contribute to this particular book, which features so many wonderful and important individuals. Kim is a member of the SCBWI. Her work is on display on her website: kimwoodstudio.com

Laura Davidson ("Remembering the Ladies" logo for cover, Alice Paul)
Laura Davidson is a recent Cornell graduate in a degree in architecture, who also highly enjoys design and drawing. She is a certified Passive House consultant with PHIUS and intends to become a licenced architect and continue work in energy efficient building fields. Contact her at laadavidson@gmail.com

Laura Leigh Myers (Carrie Chapman Catt, Jeannette Rankin, Margaret Chase Smith)
Laura Leigh Myers earned her BFA in Visual Communication from the nation's oldest private art college, The Maryland Institute College of Art. She holds an MSDE Certification in Art Education, and teaches for Art With A Heart, a non-profit arts organization in Baltimore City. She shares her home with two creative children, and two cats that love to step on her artwork. Email her at: Burnsfamily4@yahoo.com

Lena Shiffman (Betty Friedan)
Lena Shiffman was born and raised in Sweden. As long as she can remember she was either reading or painting. She has illustrated many books through the years and received the Christopher Award in 1989 for her first book *Keeping a Christmas Secret* by Phyllis Reynolds Naylor. Lena attended Spectrum Institute of Commercial Art in NJ, and later studied at The Parsons School of Design and the Art Students League in New York City. She is a member of the Society of Children's Book Writers and Illustrators (SCBWI) and a former council member of the Rutgers University Council on Children's Literature (RUCCL). She lives with her family in Flemington, NJ where you can still find her either reading or painting. You can view her work at lenashiffman.com

Leslie Simon (Madeleine Albright)

Lynnor Bontigao (Sandra Day O'Connor)
Lynnor Bontigao is an illustrator based in NJ. She is a member of SCBWI (Society of Children's Book Writers and Illustrators) and is one of the founding members of the PuddleJump Collective, an international group of authors/illustrators dedicated to making a contribution to the kidlit world. Lynnor graduated with a Fine Arts degree from the University of the Philippines. She joined her family in the US permanently in 1996. She also worked as a Programmer Analyst for 15 years in the financial industry. During the summer, she holds art classes

to neighborhood kids ranging in ages 7-14. Lynnor also enjoys cooking and she can make a mean guacamole. Follow her at: lynnorbontigao.com and facebook.com/lynnorbontigaoillustrator

Mariya Kovalyov (Cover Designer, Rose Schneiderman)
Mariya Kovalyov is an artist and photographer who loves living in New Jersey with her family and an unusually large amount of dogs. She runs Happyfamilyart.com. There you can find art tutorials, crafts, more coloring pages and more about the places they visit.

Mary Delaney Connelly (Elizabeth Caty Stanton, Ida Bell Wells-Barnett, Mary Church Terrell)
Mary Delaney Connelly was born in Richmond Hill, NY in 1951. She studied textile design at FIT in NYC and worked as a designer in the textile design business then attended Queens college for fine arts. She obtained a BFA in Painting from SUNY New Paltz NY. Besides teaching art to children and adults, Mary has had numerous solo and group art shows throughout the Hudson Valley region in upstate NY. Mary currently resides in High Falls NY and continues to work at her art in various mediums. To contact please email at mgdc123@aol.com

Monisha Kulkarni (Susan B. Anthony)

Natalie Obedos (Nellie Bly, Dolores Huerta)
Natalie Obedos is currently a full-time high school senior attending her school's animation program. She is a member of the National Art Honors Society. She hopes to study animation in college and eventually work as a storyboard artist in the animation field. Website: yellowfences.tumblr.com, instagram.com/bluebasements. Contact: BlueBasements@gmail.com she likes naming her websites after colored parts of the average home and is a feminist ;))

Rachel Wintemberg (Rosa Parks)
Rachel Wintemberg teaches art at Samuel E. Shull Middle School in Perth Amboy NJ. She is the owner of the blog The Helpful Art Teacher, thehelpfulartteacher.blogspot.com/p/the-art-of-rachel-wintembe.html. Mrs. Wintemberg has illustrated several children's books and has also published many articles on the subject of art education. She holds a BFA from Pratt Institute and an MA in studio art from Montclair State University. She lives in New Jersey with her husband, daughter and two cats.

Sheryl Depp (Emma Lazarus, Marian Wright Edelman, Barbara Jordan)
Sheryl Depp is an elementary art teacher in Pasco County, Florida. She has been published in School Arts Magazine and writes the blog primarilyartwithmrsdepp.blogspot.com. Sheryl is also an active member and presenter at the FAEA and NAEA. She has been married forever and has two children and six grandchildren.

Tiffany Castle (Eliza Pinckney)

Tish Wells (Lady Bird Johnson, Inez Mulholland, Geraldine Ferraro)
Tish Wells graduated Pratt Institute with a B.A. in illustration and is now a researcher, journalist, and photographer who has worked for McClatchy, Knight-Ridder, and USA Today. Website: TishWells14.com

Victoria Ford (Martha Washington, Frances Wright, Margaret Fuller, Matilda Joslyn Gage, Maria W. Stewart, Patsy Mink, 1913 Suffrage March, 2012 Ms. Magazine)
Victoria Ford is a journalist living on Long Beach Island with her young son, Robert. A lifelong lover of drawing, and all art forms and creative pursuits, while in high school she attended workshops in figure drawing and illustration at Philadelphia's University of the Arts and Moore College of Art and Design. She furthered her art education and earned a bachelor's degree in print communications at Beaver College (since renamed Arcadia University) in Glenside, Pa. Inspired by human physicality, sensuality and emotion, she strives to capture the essence of personhood in all her work. Contact her at: thevictoriaford@gmail.com

About the poet:

Zack Applewhite (author of **They called it "Freedom"**) is a poet and a tabletop game designer and the creator of the $1 Poem Project: kickstarter.com/projects/bettagames/the-1-poem-project   facebook.com/bettagameshq

About the Author:

Carol Simon Levin is a Youth Services Librarian, author, storyteller and program presenter based in Bridgewater New Jersey. Whether she is impersonating the woman who helped to build the Brooklyn Bridge, telling the amazing stories of early women in aviation, engaging families in a rousing Halloween Hootenany of songs and stories, expanding on the mathematical and artistic possibilities of a simple square, or sharing the story of a dolphin who learned to swim with an artificial tail (along with activities to help children understand what it is like to live with a disability), she always strives to create exciting programs that engage her audience's interests and expand their horizons. She is happy to bring her presentations to libraries, senior centers, historical societies, schools, camps and other venues.

She has always been particularly fascinated by the history of technology and women's history. Visit **tellingherstories.com** or **facebook.com/TellingHerStories** for more information on her books and presentations. Additional programs and resources for children and teachers can be found at: **carolsimonlevin.blogspot.com**. Carol Simon Levin is a member of the New Jersey Library Association, the New Jersey Storytelling Guild, and the Society of Children's Book Writers and Illustrators.

Some people see things as they are
and say why.
I dream things that never were
and say why not?

—

George Bernard Shaw

Index

Made in the USA
Middletown, DE
26 January 2017